The Dads & Daughters
Togetherness Guide

Also by Joe Kelly

*Dads & Daughters: How to Inspire, Understand, and
Support Your Daughter*

The Pocket Idiot's Guide to Being an Expectant Father

The Pocket Idiot's Guide to Being a New Dad

The Body Myth: Adult Women and the Pressure to Be Perfect
(with Dr. Margo Maine)

Clean: A New Generation in Recovery Speaks Out (with Chris Beckman)

The Dads & Daughters Togetherness Guide

54 Fun Activities for Fathers and Daughters

JOE KELLY

A Lark Production

Broadway Books
New York

BROADWAY

PUBLISHED BY BROADWAY BOOKS

Copyright © 2007 by Dads & Daughters®

All Rights Reserved

Published in the United States by Broadway Books, an imprint of The Doubleday Broadway Publishing Group, a division of Random House, Inc., New York.
www.broadwaybooks.com

BROADWAY BOOKS and its logo, a letter B bisected on the diagonal, are trademarks of Random House, Inc.

The Dads & Daughters logo is a registered trademark of Dads & Daughters.

Book design by Diane Hobbing of Snap-Haus Graphics

LIBRARY OF CONGRESS CATALOGING-IN-PUBLICATION DATA
Kelly, Joe, 1954–
    The dads & daughters togetherness guide : 54 fun activities for fathers and daughters / Joe Kelly.
        p. cm.
    1. Fathers and daughters. I. Title. II. Dads and daughters togetherness guide.

    HQ755.8.K446 2007
    306.874'2—dc22

                                                                2006025612

ISBN: 978-0-7679-2469-6

PRINTED IN THE UNITED STATES OF AMERICA

10 9 8 7 6 5 4 3 2 1

FIRST EDITION

To Michael Kieschnick:
good dad, fathering visionary,
and Founder of Dads & Daughters

Contents

Introduction

A father's impact on a daughter is astounding—just ask the adult women you know. But our culture doesn't pay much attention to that influence, or to much else about father-daughter relationships. That's why, back in 1999, Michael Kieschnick and I created the world's first nonprofit dedicated to the power and potential of father-daughter relationships: Dads & Daughters®. Thousands of fathers are now part of the Dads & Daughters network, and many of them were eager to contribute ideas to this *Dads & Daughters Togetherness Guide*.

Why do fathers and stepfathers need an organization (or books) about raising daughters? Because we were all raised as sons; we are often in the dark about what it's like to be a girl. This is why we sometimes have trouble understanding how they tick!

Despite this, you are a powerful beacon for your daughter as she walks down her life road. Your example and involvement can light her way with clear and healthy expectations for men. But if your light isn't shining brightly on her childhood, she may be left lost in tangled underbrush, confused about what to accept from men. Our daughters and stepdaughters are naturally drawn toward men who choose paths similar to the ones we tread as men and fathers.

We must be an integral part of our daughters' lives, showing them our strong, supportive, and nurturing masculinity. Our example is the road map our daughters use to discover relationships (romantic or not) with boys and men we'd be proud to have as friends, sons, and brothers.

Dads and Play

Children grow up loving to play. That makes playing with your daughter a fabulous way to connect with her interests and be a potent, positive force in her life.

As grown men, our lives are often filled with stress and demands, leaving little room for "childish" play. If you're a father who doesn't live with your children or stepchildren, there can be added layers of difficulty—ranging from problems with your ex to the logistical complexity inherent in separated and blended families. We fathers sometimes have difficulty finding ways to play with our children because we aren't kids anymore.

The way we learned to play as boys can also complicate our approach to playing with daughters. We tend to see every activity (even play) as directed toward some quantifiable goal. When we play a game or a sport, we want to compete fiercely—because we want to win! When playing with our kids, those attitudes can translate into insisting on producing the "right" result: winning the game, making a bigger treehouse than the neighbor's, sticking unswervingly to the rules, and so on.

But that's not always the most constructive approach. In his book *Live-Away Dads: Staying a Part of Your Children's Lives When They Aren't a Part of Your Home* (Penguin, 1999), psychologist and fathering author William Klatte writes that making play too competitive or structured can interfere with having fun—and fun is the most important immediate goal in playing with your daughter:

> *When playing games with your children, please pay attention to* The One and Only Very Important Number One Game Rule:
> *Stop having so many rules!*
> *Rules can really be a drag when you are trying to have fun. Don't get mad if your children want to change the rules in the middle of the game. Let them. Play with them. It's only a game. Teens may want to play by rules a lot of the time, but many kids often prefer to forget the rules or make up their own. Young kids just love to win, and they'll work hard to arrange any possible way to do so.*
> *We live by rules so often at work and other parts of our adult lives that we forget to be spontaneous. If your child wants to make up her own illogical rules to a board game or card game, let her!*
> *You have plenty of opportunities to teach your child about fair play and honesty in life, and those qualities are extremely important, but it is also important to sometimes be silly, laugh, and forget*

about doing things the "right" way. Many times, the best way to do that is forget the rules and just let go.

These principles are not limited to games with formal rules, like Chutes and Ladders or Old Maid; they apply to all fun father-daughter activities. Fun play is simply essential in building a solid father-daughter connection.

When fathers and daughters play, they are at their most open and authentic. Play breaks down barriers between you, creating an ongoing opportunity to communicate and impart the treasure of your creativity, affection, and willingness to take risks—the rich heritage of your masculinity.

While bringing you two closer together, play also makes great memories—another marvelous heritage for both of you to have.

All of this holds true for fathers who want to spend quality time with their older daughters and stepdaughters, too. It is just as possible (and important) to do fun activities with girls in their teens, and this collection of activities will show you how.

Having fun means enjoying shared activity, not having "fun" at the other person's expense. You have to trust someone in order to have fun with them. As a parent, you soon learn that trust is the mortar holding together every solid relationship. This trust is necessary in your father-daughter relationship as well as in the relationship your daughter has with herself.

Your daughter learns this trust in large part through her relationship with her parents. When you are attentive and supportive, she will recognize her own strength, value, and talent, giving her the boldness, passion, and savvy to grow into a marvelous woman of whom you are justly proud.

You have incredible influence on how your stepdaughter or daughter sees herself. With your positive words and support, she can be safe and healthy, and can thrive no matter where life takes her.

That's why it's so important for all of us fathers and stepfathers to show and tell our daughters that we believe they are capable of anything! Fathering a daughter with love, respect, and fun ensures that she will choose people and situations that nourish her long after she's left our house. There's no greater legacy for us to leave our daughters.

These are some of the many "serious" reasons to have fun with your daughter. But, as Klatte reminds us, we have to keep things in perspective:

> *Playing is supposed to be fun! And I don't mean just intellectual fun and polite banter (although that certainly has its place). I mean hand-slapping, eye-watering, burst-out-laughing, forget-what-you're-doing, pee-in-your-pants, doesn't-matter-who-wins silliness! It's not always easy for dads to have fun. But it's a great goal. Allow yourself to let go when you can—both for your sake and your child's. Take humor seriously (Ha!).*

Never forget that playing is one of parenting's primary perks. It's revitalizing and renewing. It takes us out of ourselves. Most of all, playing is fun! So welcome to the *Dads & Daughters Togetherness Guide*. Dig in and start having a great time!

Tip: Many of the activities in this book can be enjoyed by mothers, stepmothers, sons, stepsons, cousins, uncles, grandparents, aunts, and anyone else who enjoys positive, fun interaction between adults and kids. We put the focus on dads and daughters because fathers often tell us that they need specific, concrete ideas on how to get—and stay—actively engaged in their daughters' lives.

You'll also notice these "Tips" throughout the book. They provide extra bits of encouragement and perspective.

Will This Work?

A book of father-daughter activities is great, at least in theory. But will it work in practice? What happens when you ask your daughter if she wants to do something together with you? After she reaches a certain age, she's liable to say things like:

I'm busy.
I'm not interested.
I've got other plans.
Can we do it some other time?
Booooring!
(Or maybe she says nothing at all and just rolls her eyes.)

Well, if this happens to you, rest assured that it isn't unusual. Every father I know has gotten responses like this from his daughter or step-daughter at least a few times (and I'm willing to bet you twenty dollars that the same holds true for every father I don't know, too). There are two important lessons to learn from this:

You're not alone.
Her reluctance isn't the last word.

So how do you get over the hump of her resistance and/or your un-certainty about whether she even *wants* to do things together with you? And what if she's wary because you haven't been super-involved in her life before and are now "suddenly" showing an interest?
There are two general approaches to this problem:

Play the parent card.
Find ways for her to take the lead.

The Parent Card

Many stepfathers and fathers I meet say they sometimes feel awkward or overwhelmed when interacting with their daughters. This is normal. Unfortunately, in our present-day culture, we've been sold the idea that there is something wrong with us if we ever feel uncomfortable. We might debate whether or not unpleasant feelings are endemic to the human condition, but there is no doubt that feeling awkward or overwhelmed is a regular part of being a parent. That's just the way it is.

But discomfort, no matter how—well, awkward—it makes us feel, is not a good reason to pull back or cop out on our job as the father of our children and stepchildren. Indeed, it is by working through the discomfort that we build the deeper parent-child connections that we and our children seek.

Of course, the person primarily responsible for leading the way through the discomfort is you, the parent. Why? Because you're the grown-up and your daughter is the kid. What does that mean for effectively using the *Dads & Daughters Togetherness Guide*?

It means that sometimes—probably more at the beginning than later on—you will have to act like a parent. When you propose doing an activity together, and she says, "I'm not interested," you assert your parental prerogative. You say something like, "That may be. But we are going to spend time doing something together anyway. I'm your dad, and I think it's important, so we're going to do it."

Don't barge in and say, "We're gonna start having fun, and begin right this very minute!" Respect her life, and schedule your dad-daughter activities ahead of time. Scheduling ahead is always a good idea; after all, that's how we usually arrange things with our adult friends and colleagues. It is especially important at the beginning if you are a dad who is (in her eyes) "suddenly" getting involved.

After you've done a few activities together, both of you will eventually start feeling comfortable having more spontaneous fun. Don't rush it, but rather think of the fun (spontaneous or planned) as its own reward.

Don't yell, snap, be rude, or overbearing—this is a book about play, not punishment. If she does indeed have a previous commitment, reschedule your activity time. But don't back down just because it's awkward. Then, keep your word. Be firm with yourself and with her, so you both know that you are serious about your commitment to spend time having fun with her. Believe it or not, that last sentence isn't oxymoronic.

Basically, this method boils down to "I'm the dad and you're the daughter, so we're going to go play."

Let Her Lead

The second method is not mutually exclusive from the first, but it is a way to stimulate your daughter's interest in initiating father-daughter activities. Ideally, we want our daughters to be eager to do things with us. When they are younger, they may seem to display such eagerness relentlessly.

But if the eagerness isn't so spontaneous, here are a couple of ideas for getting her jazzed about—or at least getting her more invested in—father-daughter activities.

The first way is to make a Dad & Daughter Activity Jar, for which you'll find instructions on page 169.

The second way to get her to buy into participating in father-daughter activities is by negotiating a contract for fun. Sounds weird, but my lawyer cousin Frank (who also happens to be one of the best divorced fathers around) assures me that you can make a contract for just about anything. There's a simple and enjoyable way to create such a contract on page 91, in what we call the Little Rock Exercise.

> **Tip:** The first few times you schedule and do a father-daughter activity together, one or both of you may feel awkward. That's okay. Admit your discomfort, but tell her that you're willing to go through discomfort because spending time with her is so important to you. If you keep doing activities together—especially if you do them regularly—then the awkwardness will quickly diminish and eventually disappear. So let the fun begin!

How The Dads & Daughters Togetherness Guide *Is (Loosely) Organized*

The Dads & Daughters Togetherness Guide aims to foster a relaxed and playful approach to your unique father-daughter playtime. That's why the subtitle has the word "fun" in it! We thought about calling it *The Dads & Daughters Activity Workbook,* but that sounded way too serious. Doing things together with our daughters and stepdaughters doesn't have to feel like work. It is too much fun!

In that spirit, we've organized the book freely and lightheartedly—because that's how we want you to use it.

There are more than fifty "chapters" in *The Dads & Daughters Togetherness Guide.* Most of these describe one father-daughter activity in detail. Others feature a kind of activity where you can choose from a couple of variations.

Some are designed for a father-daughter pair to do together alone—"solo" activities. Some are designed to be done in groups of father-daughter pairs. Dads have done these "group" activities through parent-teacher organizations, Girl Scout troops, faith communities, neighborhoods, and family reunions. A few *Togetherness Guide* activities are well suited for both solo and group settings. The solo and/or group designation appears at the beginning of each activity.

Activities are broken into four sections, roughly according to the age of the daughter:

Daddy's Little Girl
Grade School
Tweens (roughly middle school age)
Teens

At the beginning of each activity, I list what age level is most likely to enjoy it, although you will see that a few of the activities are as well suited for a six-year-old as they are for an eighteen-year-old. So be sure to read every section, no matter how old your daughter is! For example, you will find some six-to-fourteen-year-old activities in the Teen section. You and your daughter should also feel *completely* free to adapt any activity to your own needs, even if it means tossing aside the suggested age guidelines. Remember, we're taking a loose and playful approach here!

Seven chapters are called "Fast Fun," which list numerous activities but without detailed instructions (because the activities are self-explanatory). Fast Fun covers old, reliable activities you can use as warm-ups, jump-starts, or as fallbacks on those days when you feel stumped.

Throughout the book you will also find pictures of rectangular game cards. These come from one of my favorite games, Gary Burns's Com-mu-ni-ca-tion—Dads & Daughters Edition, which helps fathers and daughters break the ice and stimulate interesting discussions. Use these questions and topics to have interesting conversations with your daughter while doing any of the activities in the book—and let them lead you to explore other fascinating topics and questions.

What are you waiting for? Start browsing and having fun!

Daddy's Little Girl

Human beings accelerate through the greatest number of developmental changes in the shortest period of time before age eight. Take language acquisition as one example.

Have you ever learned (or attempted to learn) a second language? For most people it takes years of dedicated effort just to reach basic proficiency. Your daughter masters her language in just two or three years while also learning other remarkably difficult things—like how to feed herself, walk, understand cause and effect, and more. And that's just for starters.

Infants, toddlers, and young children can learn this vast array of skills and information because their minds are flexible, open (yes, even two-year-olds!), and hypercurious. This way of being also makes most children very receptive to and skilled at playing!

Your fatherly key to successful play with the preschool crowd is to adopt and reflect your daughter's flexible, open, hypercurious attitude. Embrace how creatively she connects the dots between point A and point Q. Avoid using playtime to enforce rules, make a point, or impose gender stereotypes.

During your daughter's early years, she doesn't think of herself as "a girl." Gender concepts come soon enough, often with attendant baggage. Now is the time to celebrate and reinforce her value as an individual person, not specifically as a girl. Encouraging intellectual curiosity and physical activity is especially important. Later on, when the gender straightjacket attempts to exert its influence on her, she'll need to feel comfortable in her body and confident in her brain and heart.

1. Our Time

All Ages / Solo

Psychologist and author Dr. Margo Maine wrote a fabulous book called *Father Hunger*. I think her metaphor is an ideal one for stepdads and dads to remember—our daughters hunger for our attention, no matter how young or old they are. And, let's be honest, we hunger for our daughters' attention, too!

Spending time with your daughter or stepdaughter is the best way to let her know you are paying attention to her.

Set aside some inviolate time for you and your daughter to be together without interruption. Having a daily "Our Time" is ideal, but it works on a weekly basis, too (or anywhere in between).

One divorced dad I know has shared custody of his young daughter. Since she's not always with him, he knows the value of Our Time.

To make the most of my time with my 6-year-old daughter, I organized our evenings so that the half hour before bedtime is Our Time. During Our Time, I brush my daughter's shower-wet hair and we might simply watch TV, or play a game. Our current favorites are Who Took the Cookie from the Cookie Jar, Candy Land, and Uno. We also talk about school or why some kids are bad or why people lie or something she saw that bothered her, or whatever. Mostly, we talk.

A few weeks ago, I began to think that Our Time felt forced and decided to simply not say anything. Shower time came and went, and I said nothing about Our Time. Fifteen minutes hadn't passed before my daughter approached me with brush in hand to ask what was wrong. "Daddy, why aren't we having Our Time?" I almost teared up as I said to her that we will ALWAYS have Our Time. My hope is that Our Time will grow to become a time for her to share with me what's on her mind—her fears, concerns, worries, passions, etc.—a time for us to truly bond. Granted she's only six now, but I can hope that Our Time will last forever!!

The point is that dad and daughter are together and that daughter knows that during Our Time, no phone calls, work, or other distractions will interrupt. She has Dad totally to herself. Even thirty minutes can feed the hunger a dad and a daughter have for each other. So make it a habit!

Remember that Our Time can happen even if dad and daughter are not in the same place. If you live or work away from your daughter, set aside regular Our Time during which you:

- Talk to each other on the phone or over a free Internet telephony system like Skype or Google Talk.
- IM or e-mail each other.
- Play an interactive online game together.
- Communicate with each other over Ham radio (you can even use Morse code).

Get creative and come up with your own ideas, too.

In other words, don't let distance interfere with Our Time. Fortunately, there are constantly expanding ways to communicate and connect over distances. Make them work for you!

Did you know? Eleanor Abbott of San Diego invented the Candy Land game in the 1940s to amuse herself while she recovered from polio. The first games sold for a dollar, and more than 40 million of them have been sold since!

2. Fast Fun for Daughters through Three Months

Birth to Three Months / Solo

Fast Fun is a list of activity ideas that a pop, father, dad, padre, pappa, or daddy-o can pull out any time. They don't require a lot of preparation or explanation. But if you're stumped for ideas of what to do today, this list can get you started.

When you bring your daughter home from the hospital, you are hypersensitive and may be afraid she will break if you handle her wrong. Well, that's a good thing—a father's natural instinct is to meet the needs of this completely dependent little creature. You may feel like you're on an emotional roller coaster (because you are), but you can still play and have fun with your baby.

The following suggestions are only starters. You have a lot more ideas inside you—be creative, loosen up, and most important have fun! She'll love it, and so will you.

Make faces at each other.
Let her grip your finger with her hand.
Blow very lightly on her face.
Very gently and slowly stretch her arms to her sides.
Make googlie sounds and watch her smiles.
Massage her feet and hands.
Sing softly to her.
Watch her eyes move in response to you.

Tip: I'm not a big fan of parents (or other adults) using "baby talk" all the time with babies. Make funny sounds, be lyrical and musical with your voice—but also make conversation with your baby in your normal tone of voice. She wants to get to know you: your sound, smell, expressions, and the comfort of snuggling up against you to fall asleep. Talk like you normally do and she'll get to know you faster.

3. Fast Fun for Daughters from Six Months to One Year

Six Months to One Year / Solo

As toddlers get more independent, they get more willful—and more creative, silly, adventurous, and fun. When our twins were born, people told us that the "terrible twos" would be exponentially awful because we'd have two two-year-olds at once. Well, two and three turned out to be a blast! The lesson for me was: Don't let other people's expectations determine your own unique experience with your own unique daughter.

The following suggestions are here to jump-start you. You have a lot more ideas inside you—be creative, loosen up, and most of all, remember to spend this time having fun!

Make goofy faces at each other.
Play peekaboo.
Play in the bathtub.
Take her to the store with you.
Read picture books.
Play patty-cake.
Crawl around on the floor together.
Pound on boxes.
Hide in boxes.
Mimic sounds back and forth.
Roll a ball back and forth.
Play in the sand.
Go on a picnic together.

4. Story Time
Four to Eighteen / Solo

Everybody loves a good tale, whether it's tall or very, very short. Creating and writing stories together is great fun and can tap into your best inventive, inspired imagination. Plus, this activity grows with your daughter—you can make up stories together, no matter how old she is. As the years pass, the tales tend to get longer and more interesting—and no less fun. Below are some simple ways to start.

Don't get bogged down in "traditional" rules about plot, characters, or even logic when creating stories with your daughter. There is no "wrong" direction for the stories to take. Cut loose and have fun, even if logic has completely left the premises.

Below are some simple ways to start Story Time.

The Talking Story Riff

Pick a topic, any topic. Then simply start telling a story about it. After about a minute of riffing on the story, turn it over to your daughter and listen closely to where she takes the characters and plot. After another minute, she tosses the story back to you, to add your next minute of detail and plot. Back and forth you go, wherever your joint imaginations and the characters lead you.

Keep in mind that the first few times you do this activity, it may seem a little flat. And the first few exchanges in any particular story may (or may not) be a little flat. Don't sweat it or think you're failing. Instead, think of these initial efforts as first drafts. Many professional writers tear up nearly every first draft—we do first drafts to get the pump primed and the juices flowing.

When our daughters were ten, we drove from northern Minnesota to Disney World and back, with some detours to visit relatives, friends, and historic sites in Atlanta. That trip was the first time the girls ever saw a Waffle House restaurant (a fixture in Southeastern states), and they were fascinated—because they loved waffles. So when we started making up a fairy tale in the car, it became known as "The Waffle Story," starring Ann Tellet, a work colleague of my wife's who took a real shine to the kids. In "The Waffle Story," Ann solved mysteries and went on adventures. Her biggest adventure was into the world of dinettes. Why? Because we drove past a store that was called (really!) World of Dinettes.

My point is: There is nothing too silly, illogical, spontaneous, or tangential to include in a talking story riff. Run with it as long as it feels like you're both still being creative and stimulated. Long road trips are a great time to trot this activity out. You may have so much fun that you and your daughters will remember that story decades later!

Tag-Team Telling

This is basically a written variation of the Talking Story Riff. Instead of creating the story out loud, take turns advancing the plot on paper.

Let your daughter start writing down the story and, depending on her age, have her pass it over to you after she's completed a paragraph or a page. Then you take it for a paragraph or a page. Be sure you are completing entries of about the same length as hers, so that you don't start dominating the story.

Tag-Team Telling is often more flexible than making up a story out loud. For example, live-away dads can Tag-Team a story with their daughters through e-mail, snail mail, or during the times they spend together in person.

Even when you live with your daughter or stepdaughter, you can have one or more Tag-Team Telling stories under way for days, weeks, months—or even years. Just be sure that the paper (or computer document) is where you and she can both access it readily—in case either one or both of you come up with an inspiration in the middle of the night or middle of the day.

Picture Books

Readers of just about every age like illustrations in their storybooks. Go ahead and draw pictures or take photographs to accompany the tale you and she are creating together. Her drawings can be wonderful and fun, and also give you insight into her images of the characters, environment, and story line.

You can even tag-team illustrations! For example, here's a wild way to draw a character:

- Fold a piece of paper in thirds.
- Have her draw the character's head on one third, while you look away (no peeking). When she's done, she folds that third of the paper over so you can't see the details.
- You then draw the character's torso and arms on the middle third of the paper (no peeking by your daughter), then fold it over so she can't see your contribution.
- Then, she takes back the paper and draws the legs and feet on its final third. When she's done, unfold the paper and see what wacky and creative images you have drawn together!

You can also share illustration duties in a slightly less chaotic manner. For example, you can alternate drawings to accompany your joint story, or else each of you can take photographs to use in illustration.

The possibilities are endless, as long as you stay in touch with your three I's: Invention, Inspiration, Imagination.

5. *Your Own Private Camp*
Four to Ten / Solo

My wife once said, "A good test of how good a friend you are with someone is whether you can still stand each other after going camping together." Yes, like most things that change the pace of our daily routine, camping can bring out the best in us, or something else.

However, one of the best things about camping is that you can do it almost anywhere—including your own backyard. Plus, it doesn't have to be complicated or cost a fortune.

The essentials for backyard camping are:

> Tent or screen-house to keep out the rain and bugs
> Sleeping bags, whether store-bought or create-your-own
> Flashlight (to find your way back to the house)
> Snacks

See how short that list is? You can use an old tent from the garage, or borrow one from a friend. You can use any sleeping bag (even the one from back when you were a Boy Scout), or else make your own by folding up a couple of blankets, wrapping them in a sheet, and then layering other blankets on top for a cozy place to sleep.

The most important elements of backyard camping are the rituals you develop together. Make sure the two of you work together to put up the tent, arrange the sleeping bags, pick out the snacks, and so on. It probably won't qualify as "roughing it" (after all, a fully plumbed bathroom is only steps away), but that's not the point. The idea is to break up your usual routine, do something out of the ordinary together, and see what develops.

If it's safe, build a small campfire and roast marshmallows while you sit around it and talk. You can even just fire up a charcoal grill to serve the same function.

To make the traditional camp snack "s'mores," roast a marshmallow until its center begins to liquefy. Then quickly insert it between two graham crackers along with a thin piece of chocolate candy bar. The chocolate starts to melt as you pop the whole sweet, messy delicacy in your mouth. Mmmmm!

Make sure to do other traditional camp things like singing songs, telling tall tales, and sharing "scary" stories. Sit or lie on the grass and look at the moon and stars. Stay up late and just chat with each other.

Odds are that the memories you both create in your own backyard will outlast any that come from going away to camp.

> **Tip:** You can easily create a camplike experience indoors by pinning and draping blankets over pieces of furniture, then snuggling underneath for the night. Such homemade "forts" make great places to play no matter what time of day or season.

Grade School

As your daughter heads off to school, she gradually increases her independence from you. Activities, responsibilities, and interests outside your home slowly begin to take up more of her time and attention.

They take up more of your attention, too, as you juggle schedules, carpools, shopping, meals, and homework in order to help her life run smoothly and help her grow. Sometimes this hubbub overwhelms some essentials of parenting and family life, like spending time together without the intrusion of other responsibilities or distractions.

The more time your daughter spends outside the family—at school, sports, and after-school activities—the more she is exposed to the influence of our wider culture. Some of that influence is positive for girls and some of it is negative. In my book *Dads & Daughters: How to Inspire, Understand, and Support Your Daughter* (Broadway, 2003), I talk in detail about these influences and the incredible, positive leverage we fathers and stepfathers can have if we are actively involved in our daughters' lives.

So during your daughter's grade school years, make sure you keep setting aside special "dad and daughter" togetherness time. School and extracurricular activities are important—but so is time and space to keep building a solid daughter-father relationship. If you dedicate yourself to togetherness time now, you'll both be much better prepared for the squalls that lie ahead in the "tween" and teen years.

Besides, plenty of fun father-daughter togetherness activities are also great learning opportunities, which make them a perfect supplement to your daughter's formal education. Think creatively about spending time together, and then make sure you actually spend the time. Time with your daughter has to be invested today in order to reap the returns you want down the road.

6. The Dad & Daughter Private Journal

Five to Eighteen / Solo

Many memories, great and small, get lost because we don't record them. A Dad & Daughter Private Journal (or DDPJ) is one great way to scoop up memories and thoughts for safekeeping.

We recommend using one journal that you both write in. You can have separate sections within the book for each of you, or just write in a rolling back-and-forth fashion from front to back!

Here are some pointers:

1. Decorate the cover of your DDPJ (together) before you start. Follow her artistic lead and use her "art" tools, be they crayons, photos, or oil paints. If you keep up your DDPJ, you will soon move into multiple volumes—and more opportunities for artistic expression on the covers!

2. When beginning your DDPJ, agree that you will each write in it at least once a day, every day, for the first month. This will get you in the rhythm, and reinforce how valuable and fun the activity is.

3. Make a contract to keep using the DDPJ for a set period of time. Be brave—sign up for at least a year! (You'll get hooked and want to do it forever.)

4. Be creative. If you want to, use some DDPJ pages to express yourselves in drawing, collages, photographs, poetry, tall tales, or whatever else you dream up.

5. Be honest about how you feel, but always write lovingly and with respect.

6. Remember to record all the things you do together.

7. Remember to record things about the other person that you admire, find fun, and that inspire you.

8. Date your entries with the month, day, and year—you'll be glad you did.

9. Use the DDPJ to encourage her and express your love, not to reprimand or lecture her.

10. If you have trouble thinking of something to write, pick a letter of the alphabet and write out all of her best qualities that start with that letter. "You are Responsible, Refreshing, Reliable, a Raconteur, have great Rapport with your little brother. . . ."

Some alternative methods of keeping a DDPJ:
1. Each of you keeps their own journal, dedicated just to memories, reflections, thoughts, and feelings about the other person. You share these journals with each other at least once a week.
2. Leave messages on Post-it notes around the house for each other, and then collect them in your DDPJ.
3. E-mail your journal entries to each other, and then take turns being responsible for printing them out and saving them—perhaps in a wonderfully decorated three-ring binder. (Good for live-away dads and fathers who have to travel a lot.)
4. Record audio messages to each other on a tape recorder or computer. Then you can replay each other's voices over and over. Try to save the messages digitally, so the quality doesn't degrade over time. (Again, good for live-away dads and fathers who travel a lot.)

One dad I know started his own daughter journal from very early on:

I have been keeping a journal of my thoughts related to my first daughter since she was born, and hope to keep doing so as long as I can. My hope is that I keep it up and give it to her as a gift when she goes away to college. I decided to do this so she knows her dad's thoughts throughout her life.

Another bonus—once you get going with your DDPJ, it may quickly become a safe place for each of you to write about subjects that are hard for you to talk about out loud with each other. If something the other person writes upsets you, give yourself some time to reflect before writing a response or talking to her about it.

Tip: Remember to use your DDPJ to save creations from other activities in *The Dads and Daughters Togetherness Guide,* like Papa Poetry.

The time I felt the most loved in my life was when _____.

I say that because...

© 2004 Mindamics

A
5

7. Six Impossible Things Before Breakfast

Five to Ten / Solo

In the wonderful book *Through the Looking-Glass,* Alice (of Wonderland fame) laughs at the White Queen and tells her that "there's no use trying, one can't believe impossible things." To which the royal lady replies: "I daresay you haven't had much practice. When I was younger, I always did it for half an hour a day. Why, sometimes I've believed as many as six impossible things before breakfast." In that delightful turn of phrase, Charles Lutwidge Dodgson (aka Lewis Carroll) gave us a great game to play with our own Alices.

On a Saturday soon, take your daughter out to breakfast at a sit-down restaurant like IHOP, Perkins, or the local café. After you order, tell her that you each have to think of six impossible things before breakfast comes. Let your imagination run wild.

I've heard of daughters coming up with things like:

> Pulling up this seat cushion opens a door that takes us to China.
> I'll train my clothes to fold themselves and put themselves away in the dresser.
> When horses can fly, I want one.
> Any scene I paint will come to life when I snap my fingers.

Ask her for details of what her impossible things would look like and/or do.

You come up with your list of impossible things before breakfast, too. Let outlandish thoughts rule, and chances are you'll still be talking about your impossible things when you're walking or driving back home.

> **Tip:** Save some of your "impossible things before breakfast" lists in your DDPJ (p. 24).

8. *Museums*
Five to Eighteen / Solo and Group

If you need a preconstructed activity to do with your daughter, visit a museum. Nearly every community has one, from a small town historical society to the Getty in Los Angeles and from the Metropolitan in New York to COSI in Columbus, Ohio.

Museums cover a wide range of topics, too. If one or both of you are interested in science, art, railroads, history—or even Spam sandwich spread—there is at least one museum for you.

In our U.S. national collection of museums, the Smithsonian Institution (www.si.edu), deserves special mention. Its amazing museums along the Mall in Washington, D.C. (and also in New York City and Chantilly, Virginia) are mind-boggling in their variety and depth. Smithsonian exhibits cover Native American history, wacky inventions, classic European paintings, spaceships, and everything in between. A father and daughter could spend a month in D.C. visiting the Smithsonian and still not exhaust it. But it's still worth trying!

I've broken up the following list of museums by type, and then provided links to help you find one close to where you live or where you and your daughter might be traveling. The websites listed have tons of links and resources that can inspire the two of you for a long time.

Keep in mind that some museums are not definable by a single category. The Bishop Museum in Honolulu (www.bishopmuseum.org) is a good example; it combines science, history, and art museums (along with a planetarium) on one campus.

Children's Museums

The Association of Children's Museums (www.childrensmuseums.org) has links to kids' museums all across the U.S. as well as features on individual facilities. Many of these facilities cater to young children, so teens may want something more adult.

Art Museums

The Art Museum Network (www.amn.org/museums_000.html) lists two hundred public art collections around the United States. You have to already know the museum name to find it, though.

- The University of Michigan's "Mother of All Art History Links Page" (www.umich.edu/~hartspc/histart/mother/museums.html#unitedstates) connects you with hundreds of art facilities in North America and Europe.
- You can find kid-friendly art (and other) museums at Kids World online— www.northvalley.net/kids/museums.shtml
- The ArtCyclopedia website (www.artcyclopedia.com/education.html) has a great guide to art museums, with websites designed to entertain and educate kids with games, art interpretation, lesson plans, and the like.

According to *Child* magazine, the best art museums for younger children in 2006 were:

1. Art Institute of Chicago
2. Metropolitan Museum of Art, New York City
3. Dayton (Ohio) Art Institute
4. de Young Fine Arts Museums of San Francisco
5. Carnegie Museum of Art, Pittsburgh
6. Los Angeles County Museum of Art
7. Joslyn Art Museum, Omaha, Nebraska
8. Winterthur Museum & Country Estate, Delaware
9. Dallas Museum of Art
10. Peabody Essex Museum, Salem, Massachusetts

I've been to seven of these (which may mean that I'm still a young child), and agree that they were all fun and very approachable. They have kid-friendly staffs, places to stop and rest, food children will like, and tolerance for some of the noise and chaos children bring.

Science Museums

The Association of Science-Technology Centers (www.astc.org) lists hundreds of top-notch museums across the U.S. and the world, in places as diverse as Flint, Little Rock, Ithaca, Lincoln, Philadelphia, Hilo, Anchorage, Huntsville, Denver, Miami, Phoenix, Shreveport, both Portlands (Maine and Oregon), Ottawa, Halifax, Montreal, Newcastle upon Tyne (UK), Lahore (India), Hong Kong—you get the picture.

The Franklin Institute in Philadelphia (www.fi.edu) is the science museum I grew up visiting, but it is also a national leader in promoting girls' interests in science.

History Museums

We are blessed to live in a time and place that dedicates many resources to the study and celebration of history. Nearly every person in North America is within a fairly short drive of a historical site, society, or museum. Here are a few of my favorites:

- Independence Hall, Philadelphia (www.nps.gov/inde)
- National Women's History Museum, Washington, D.C. (www.nmwh.org)
- Women's Rights National Historical Park, Seneca Falls, New York (www.nps.gov/wori)
- National Underground Railroad Freedom Center, Cincinnati (www.freedomcenter.org)
- National Civil War Museum in Harrisburg, Pennsylvania (www.nationalcivilwarmuseum.com)
- Confederate Civil War Museum, New Orleans (www.confederatemuseum.com)
- Gettysburg National Military Park (www.nps.gov/gett/home.htm)
- The United States Holocaust Memorial Museum in Washington, D.C. (www.ushmm.org)
- National Civil Rights Museum, Memphis, Tennessee (www.civilrightsmuseum.org)
- The Museum of World War II, Natick, Massachusetts (www.museumofworldwarii.com)

- National Cowboy & Western Heritage Museum, Oklahoma City (www.nationalcowboymuseum.org)
- National Museum of the United States Air Force, Dayton, Ohio (www.wpafb.af.mil/museum)
- U.S. Army Engineer Museum, Fort Leonard Wood, Missouri (www.wood.army.mil/MUSEUM/Info/mus_info.htm)
- Dr. Martin Luther King Jr. National Historic Site, Atlanta (www.nps.gov/malu)
- Civil Rights Memorial Center, Montgomery, Alabama (www.splcenter.org/crm/crmc.jsp)

Specialty and Unusual Museums

Our society isn't interested in just art and history. We are also fascinated with technology, sports, and—sometimes—stuff that is simply weird. A small taste:

- The Spam Museum in Austin, Minnesota (www.spam.com)— yes, there really is such a place. And they hold an annual Spam Jam there.
- International Museum of the Horse in Lexington, Kentucky (www.imh.org) speaks to girls' fascination with horses.
- The Mattress Factory Art Museum in Pittsburgh, Pennsylvania (www.mattress.org) features fiber arts.
- American Computer Museum in Bozeman, Montana (www.compustory.com).
- The Museum of Communications (formerly The Vintage Telephone Equipment Museum) in Seattle (www.scn.org).
- The World Figure Skating Museum & Hall of Fame in Colorado Springs (www.worldskatingmuseum.org).
- National Baseball Hall of Fame and Museum in Cooperstown, New York (www.baseballhalloffame.org) is one of my all-time favorites, and my daughters loved it, too. Very manageable in one day for girls over ten.
- Civilian Conservation Corps Museum, Roscommon, Michigan (www.michigan.gov/hal/0,1607,7-160-17447_18595_18602-

54443--,00.html) documents the CCC, which employed thousands to build and rebuild U.S. landmarks during the Great Depression.

- The Houdini Museum in Scranton, Pennsylvania (www.houdini .org), and the Houdini Historical Center in Appleton, Wisconsin's Outagamie Museum (www.foxvalleyhistory.org/houdini/), celebrate the famous magician and escape artist.
- The National Cryptologic Museum at Fort George G. Meade, Maryland (www.nsa.gov/museum/index.cfm) includes historical machines and fascinating stories about spying.
- The Circus Hall of Fame in Peru, Indiana (www.circushallof fame.com).
- The Circus World Museum and Ringlingville in Baraboo, Wisconsin (www.wisconsinhistory.org/circusworld).
- The Circus Museum at John and Marie Ringling Museum of Art in Sarasota, Florida (www.ringling.org/circus_museum.asp).
- The Rails Museums Worldwide website (www.railmuseums.com) honors truth in advertising; it has listings for exhibits worldwide.
- Lake Superior Railroad Museum (www.lsrm.org/Home) is in my hometown (Duluth, Minnesota), and I've been repeatedly. Can you tell who has a thing for railroad museums?

Funny "Virtual" Museums on the Web

You don't even have to leave home to visit a museum. Most major art and science museums have "virtual" museums online, many designed specifically for kids. Then there are also the fun online museums that deal exclusively with downright silly topics. A sampling:

- The Candy Wrapper Museum (www.candywrappermuseum.com) "where wrappers are to be enjoyed as art, nostalgia, and humor."
- The Incredible World of Navel Fluff (www.feargod.net/fluff.html) is based in Australia, so an online tour is probably smarter than an on-site visit.
- Toast Portraits of Famous People (www.mauricebennett.co.nz/

tart.htm) comes from New Zealand; makes you wonder about folks down under, eh?

- The Washington Banana Museum (www.bananamuseum.com), whose motto is Groucho Marx's famous line, "Time flies like an arrow; fruit flies like a banana."
- Delphion's Gallery of Obscure Patents (www.delphion.com/gallery), which includes an inflatable rug and a bird diaper (don't ask).

Tip: Some museums have far more exhibits and activities than any one person can see in one day. Remember that the museum will be there again tomorrow, so don't rush through it. Tune in to your daughter's interest and her stamina, and don't hesitate to come back for another visit, or two, or three.

Also, if you can, visit on weekdays or other times when the museum is less crowded. Big "blockbuster" exhibits may not be worth the investment of time and money when taking younger kids.

9. Eat the Bridge
Five to Ten / Solo and Group

Is it possible to combine physics and food? Or is it fysics and phood? Either way, the answer is yes.

Of course physics and chemistry are part of nearly all everyday activities like baking (see Bring Her Flours, p. 39). But you can also explore more visible physics at work by building a miniature bridge with simple (and edible) tools like pretzel sticks, gumdrops, and marshmallows.

Use the marshmallows and/or gumdrops as foundation blocks into which you stick pretzel stick "girders" to form a bridge. With younger girls, you can start out doing this just for fun. But then you can work together to create an edible bridge that can actually hold something up. Build triangles, since they are the strongest shape, and then connect your formations together to start making a bridge.

Put two cardboard boxes a few inches away from each other, and place your bridge across the gap between them. Then, test your structure by putting small crackers on it. Slowly add more weight (like additional crackers, or else cookies, bread, pieces of fruit, and so on). Each time your bridge collapses under its weight, rebuild another one, using new designs and/or additional edible elements that you think can handle the extra strain. Make sure the "floor" (we recommend the kitchen table) under the bridge is clean, so the food stays edible!

To get ideas on what might work, start by looking around the house to see what kind of "superstructure" holds up the kitchen table and chairs. Then take a drive to examine some real bridges. You can also look at photographs and books to see what makes bridges work.

If you have a postal or kitchen scale, use it to compare the weight of your bridge with the weight of what it can hold. You will soon discover the miracle of physics, which shows how a properly assembled structure can support more than its own weight.

As you get more daring with your bridges, feel free to substitute other food items—for example, hard candy sticks are sturdy girders and dense bread can make a nice foundation block. If your daughter wants to sketch out designs before building, go for it.

Eventually, you and she might want to move on to building more permanent spanning structures with more lasting materials, such as wood and metal. In some families this may actually mushroom into furniture-building (see Power Tools, p. 149).

But for this activity, stick to materials you can chew and swallow. That way, when your bridge collapses, you can eat the remains to gain strength for your next attempt!

One thing I admire the most about you is _____.

I say that because...©

10. Hair Today, There Tomorrow

Three to Twelve / Solo

Every daughter goes through phases of loving to futz with her hair—and some daughters never grow out of those phases. And just as long as girls' hair has grown, people have thought that hair was an entirely female domain.

It doesn't have to be. In fact, playing with and fixing up each other's hair can be one of the most fun and satisfying activities dads and daughters do together, especially during the younger years. And if you're worried that you can't develop the expertise, just take a look at all the men who are hairstylists and all the live-away dads who keep their kids looking presentable.

My friend Gary is a single dad who learned styling techniques first from female friends, and then from his daughter herself. Gary says:

> *If you don't know anyone, then take her to a playground and find another mom. They will love to show you. I've seen moms teach each other. It's nothing to be ashamed about. I've seen women who adopted children with challenging hair seeking help from someone with experience in the particular kind of hair. My braiding won't win awards, but it allows me to go camping or to make her presentable in public if her mom's not around.*

The best thing is to follow your daughter's lead. Keep attuned to her comfort level and patience. Below are some practical ideas on how to get into the hair game.

Practice simple hair techniques, like braiding, on your daughter's dolls. In fact, that's also a great way for her to teach you some tricks. Once you learn the simple styles like braiding, you've got an always useful skill.

To get out tangles, start at the bottom and work your way up. The more regularly you brush her hair, the less tangled it will get. Also, let her brush your hair often, too. It keeps your hair in great shape, builds connection, and feels really good, too!

If you have a preschool daughter with kinky, easily-tangled hair, start her bath by washing the hair and working conditioner into it. Then finish the rest of the bath while the conditioner soaks in. Rinse the conditioner out only at the very end of the bath.

Sometimes hair problems can get very frustrating for dad and daughter. Here is one father's suggestion: "If all else fails, have it cut. My daughter finally got tired of the hassle and asked for it to be cut off. Her mom and I waited a while but she asked several times, so it just got cut short. Not real short, but it makes this whole process a lot easier."

If she has long hair and is physically active on a regular basis (as I hope she is), encourage her to wear braids or a ponytail; they provide less fuss and more mobility. Here's another dad's advice: "Ponytails are pretty easy. The key is to be careful not to tug individual strands as you pull them through the holder. *Don't use a rubber band!* It will snag the hair and everyone will suffer. There are many kinds of stretchy holders you can get that are easy to put in and take out. Make it tight enough to hold the hair, but not so tight it hurts—she'll probably let you know if you do that!"

Getting Gum Out of Her Hair

Nearly every parent faces this dilemma at least once. Fortunately, the solution is probably in your kitchen cupboard! Rub peanut butter (smooth is better than chunky) around the gum and into her hair. Oil in the peanut butter counters the gum's stickiness, so work it in slowly, and the gum will start to come out of her hair. Some people swear by butter or mayonnaise, but peanut butter gets the most votes—plus, how often does a kid get to put food in her hair? Don't forget to shampoo the goop out when you're done, or little critters might visit her hair for a nibble.

Getting Fancy

You can get a number of ideas and tips on girls' hairstyles at www.hairfinder.com/articles2005/girlshairstyles.htm.

Klutz Books has several great books to help you and your daughter or stepdaughter learn fun new (and old) hair techniques:

Hair Wraps by Anne Akers Johnson (weaving decorative thread into hair).
Braids and Bows by Anne Akers Johnson and Robin Stoneking.
Hair: A Book of Braiding & Styles by Anne Akers Johnson.
Rainbow Hairstyles: Simple Styles with a Touch of Color by Susan Fox. Comes with bottles of brush-on, wash-out colors (Shocking Pink, Blue Blazes, etc.).
Beaded Bobby Pins by Marilyn Green. How to make stylish—but remarkably easy—hair ornaments.

Finally, check out this fun story of a dad doing his daughter's braids, at http://askpang.typepad.com/relevant_history/2004/07/braids.html.

> **Tip:** Younger girls often like to comb or brush other people's hair. Be sure to let her do yours, and don't fret about how it turns out—you can fix it later if you need to. It's not only relaxing, it's also a great chance to listen to what's on her mind. She will giggle at the chance to style *your* hair with her sparkly clips and bows. Don't worry, you don't have to leave the house (although you could!), but she'll love it if you don't remove the accessories immediately.

11. *Bring Her Flours*
Six to Sixteen / Solo

Among my favorite photos of my daughters are the ones where they are covered in a kind of white dust. At age six, they are sitting around the kitchen table "helping" Mom make bread. Their hands, clothes, faces, and hair feature multiple splotches of sticky dough and a wide distribution of flour.

I love these photos because baking was (and still is) a favorite and fun activity that we do together as a family, or (even more fun) that I could do one-on-one with a daughter. Plus, it's inexpensive!

When our girls were little we didn't have a ton of money, so we looked for cheap, enjoyable things to do together that seemed to deliver a big payoff. Baking something yummy always fit the bill.

My girls and I especially enjoyed making (and then eating) a devil's food cake recipe I adapted from a 1949 cookbook that my mother got as a wedding gift. For a long stretch we made one every weekend, and so the girls started teasing me, saying (with a wink and broad smile), "How boring. Are we gonna make chocolate cake again?" I think it was their first experience with sarcasm.

That's how my recipe came to be known as Daddy's Boring Chocolate Cake. Here's the recipe to get you started on a father-daughter baking adventure.

Daddy's Boring Chocolate Cake
Serves eight, but if you actually have eight people, make two cakes because everyone will want seconds.

Ingredients
9 tablespoons unsweetened cocoa powder
15 tablespoons butter at room temperature (one stick is eight tablespoons)
1.5 cups milk (or any combo of milk, yogurt, or buttermilk)

2.25 cups sifted cake flour
1.5 teaspoons baking soda
1.5 teaspoons baking powder
0.75 teaspoon salt
1.5 cups sugar
3 eggs, well beaten
1.5 teaspoons vanilla flavoring

Directions

• Heat oven to 350 degrees F. Grease and flour two 8-inch round cake pans.

• For the cake, melt all of the cocoa powder together with 5 tablespoons of the butter—either over low heat in a double-boiler pot on the stove, or nuke it in a bowl for less than a minute. Cover the bowl so no one complains about chocolate splatter in the microwave.

• While that mixture cools a bit, cream the remaining 10 tablespoons of butter with the back of a wooden spoon in a ceramic bowl. Okay, you can use a metal bowl or even one of those electric mixing contraptions (although that wouldn't be the way we did it when our kids were little and we were poor!). Plus, Dad gets to show how strong he is! While I remain convinced there is some special quality that results from using a wooden spoon and ceramic bowl, don't ask me to prove it. (Baking is part science, part art.)

• Add the warm, but not hot, chocolate mixture into the butter, and then mix it all together.

• Slowly add the sugar and mix together with the butter. Yes, I know, no father likes to add anything slowly, but dumping it all in at once only makes your arm tired from extra stirring.

• Add the beaten eggs, and mix them in.

• Next, alternate adding the milk/buttermilk/yogurt liquid and the dry ingredients (flour, salt, etc.) into the bowl to complete the batter.

• You are supposed to sift together the flour, baking soda, baking powder, and salt before you add it to the batter. Do it if you're a stickler for directions. I usually just add the salt, powder, and soda to the gooey batter before tossing in the flour. Fathers can take liberties like that, especially when chocolate is involved.

• When the batter is all smoothly mixed together in that hue that makes brown so beautiful, dump it into the cake pans—about half in each one. If you actually measure how much you put in each pan, you are breaking the Father's Universal Baking/Cooking Law of "Estimating is good enough."

• Bake it for 30 to 40 minutes, depending on how reliable your oven is. Test by sticking a toothpick in the center—it is done when the toothpick comes out just dry.

• Let the cakes cool in their pans on a cooling rack for about 15 minutes, then turn them out of the pans onto the cooling racks. Let the cakes cool some more, until they are no longer warm to the touch. If you let impatience out again, your frosting will melt! (Waiting until the cake is cool enough to frost is simply the hardest part of this recipe.)

White Frosting

Ingredients
3 to 4 tablespoons butter
Speck salt
3 to 4 cups of confectioner's sugar. (Or maybe more. Or maybe less. See how it goes.)
About 4 to 5 tablespoons milk
1.5 teaspoons vanilla flavoring

Directions
• Let butter soften in a mixing bowl. This again requires patience. One alternative is to play chicken with the microwave, trying to get the butter to "soften" without going over the line to "melted." Another is to leave the butter on top of an old electric nontransistor radio—the kind with tubes inside—it generates a nice low, even heat.

• If you don't own an ancient radio, another trick is putting (wrapped!) sticks of butter in your armpits, just like the Boys Scouts taught us to warm up frostbitten fingers. Be sure to wear a shirt with sleeves. Your daughter will find this pose hilarious.

• Add salt and work the butter with the back of a wooden spoon, or use a mixer on high. Good luck getting your wooden spoon to keep up with a mixer's "high."

• Gradually mix in about a third of the sugar, then alternate the milk and sugar until it is all combined.

• Mix it extremely well, until it looks fluffy. (Okay, I confess; I use an electric mixer for the frosting.) Usually you have to play around with a little more sugar here, little more liquid there. Depends on the elevation and humidity, I guess. Or maybe the karma.

• When frosting is smooth, mix in the vanilla. Now you are ready to start spreading the frosting onto the cake with a knife and/or plastic spatula. Remember, you can tell a lot about a guy by whether he puts the thickest frosting between the two layers or on the top.

Variations

Brown Chocolate Frosting
Do everything the same, but melt 9 tablespoons unsweetened cocoa powder and 3 tablespoons butter together and let it cool before adding it to the standard frosting recipe. You'll have to increase your sugar by a cup or so, and your milk by a couple of tablespoons. So not only does it taste really good, you get more of it!

Mocha Frosting
Make like the Brown Chocolate Frosting, only substitute a quarter of a cup of *very* strong coffee for the milk. A love for mocha frosting is the only reason to keep freeze-dried instant coffee in the house.

How to Eat Boring Chocolate Cake
Eat Boring Chocolate Cake with a tall glass of very cold milk. You will soon see that this cake disappears in a day. Thus, the two of you will be forced to make another one next weekend (or tomorrow), and pretty

soon the whole family will be teasing you about that "boring chocolate cake" while clamoring for just one more piece. Won't you two be proud!

Bon Appicake!

> **Tip:** Dads and daughters can cook or bake together any day of the week. Make a regular date with her to make a fancy dinner for her mom or stepmom. Explore cookbooks, the library, and the Internet for new and different recipes. Dads often take on making the weekend breakfast. If that's one of your talents, enlist your daughter's help to make it a joint tradition—one that might last a lifetime!

12. *What-Do-You-Think Wall*
Four to Eighteen / Solo

One great joy of being in a family is the conversations that spring up around the dinner table or while doing things together around the house. When our children were growing up, many a supper conversation revolved around something one of us had read in a book or newspaper (this was an eternity ago in the last century, before cell phones, blogs, or even websites—around 1990).

Conversations about the things we read and hear can develop critical thinking skills in our children, are opportunities to pass along values to them, and can help us learn more about each other. The What-Do-You-Think Wall (inspired by the MacGregor family in North Carolina) helps stimulate these kinds of conversations and observations.

With your daughter, find a wall in a high-traffic area of your home. A kitchen wall is ideal, but you can use any wall—or even the side of a large appliance like the refrigerator. This will be your What-Do-You-Think Wall.

Decide, with your daughter, what materials will work best for your wall. You can use a wipe-off board, bulletin board, flip-chart pad, or a large piece of sturdy cardboard or newsprint. The key is to make the writable surface large enough to accommodate ideas from you and your daughter (and other family members, too).

Use one part of the wall to write down or tape/pin up:

- Interesting articles you read
- Comments you hear in the media
- Comments you hear from friends, neighbors, relatives
- A passage or quotation that strikes you while reading a book
- A creative thought that just occurred to you
- A photograph from the news
- A photograph of a work of art

The rest of the wall is used for other family members to write down their responses to the things that are posted. If you're pressed for wall space, a hanging clipboard can work as the place to write down thoughts and reactions.

Rules for using the What-Do-You-Think Wall:

- No ridiculing another family member, what they post, or what they write.
- Avoid using the wall to deal indirectly with family conflict.
- Avoid using the wall to post schedules, phone numbers, messages, etc.; have another location for those bits of family logistics.

The What-Do-You-Think Wall isn't meant to be a place to come up with airtight answers, but rather to come up with interesting questions and observations. It will provide plenty of fodder for fodder (oops, I meant "father")-daughter conversations. It will also stimulate discussion among everyone in the family.

If you use the wall well, you will both be impressed by the insights you'll gain about each other and the rest of your family.

13. *Rainy Days*
Two to Twelve / Solo

Do you dread rainy or snowy weekend days when you are "stuck" in the house with your children? Well, as with most things in life, our response to rainy days with kids is mostly a matter of attitude.

Think of inclement weather as a great opportunity to snuggle into your home and focus your attention on each other as you play, play, play. When my daughters were young, I found that rainy days were most successful when large chunks of them passed with the TV off. We filled the time instead with games, projects, reading, talking, or just goofing around.

Attitude #1

The first step in a successful rainy day is asking your daughter what she'd like to do. If she wants to play dolls, then throw yourself into it and play along. You can even stretch a little and play the part of some Barbies, rather than sticking exclusively to the Kens.

A quite macho dad once told me that the biggest challenge to his manhood was getting down on the floor to play dolls with his daughter: "But I realized that it was a lot easier and safer than throwing myself in front of a bus to save her, which I knew I would do without thinking twice about it. Then, when I saw how much fun she had when Dad played dolls, I was hooked."

Attitude #2

The second step, especially with younger daughters, is letting go of the idea that every father-daughter activity and interaction has to accomplish something concrete, lasting, and measurable. Play isn't quantifiable the way other parts of our lives may be. Paradoxically, that's what makes play so valuable.

So, use rainy days to practice using cardboard boxes to make robots, houses, or forts. Who cares that the cardboard box may not survive the day intact? The accomplishment is in the playing itself.

Perhaps the most hackneyed cliché in the world is "Enjoy your kids while you can—they grow up *so* fast." After more than a quarter century of fathering, I can tell you why that cliché is so often heard: *because it's true!*

It is a truth that's hard to recognize in the everyday ebb and flow of rearing daughters. But I found rainy days to be the best times to remember the fleeting nature of youth, and to gratefully cherish this one unique day during which I could submerge myself in my daughters' child-ness.

Attitude #3

Use what's around. Chances are, you or your daughter have card games, board games, jigsaw puzzles, or craft books around your home. Get them out and use them. You can connect and talk with your daughter (and enjoy her, too) while "aimlessly" playing Crazy Eights, Uno, Chutes and Ladders, Old Maid, Monopoly—or while assembling a puzzle or letting her teach you how to crochet or weave hot pads.

You can draw pictures on the basement floor with sidewalk chalk. You can drag out old magazines and cut them up to make art projects. Or you can cut up magazines to create your own, limited-edition family newspaper with news of recent significant events, like celebrating a birthday or getting the snow tires put on.

Read a Book Together

Snuggle in (by the fire, on the floor, in a big chair) with a family-friendly chapter book. Take turns reading chapters, or you can read the whole thing. Take breaks for snacks or lunch, but then return to your book for a few more chapters together. It will make you feel like you are in your own private world for a while.

Tip: Keep track of your favorite rainy day activities in your DDPJ (see p. 24), because your daughter and you will probably want to return to them next time the weather is lousy. Plus, those created-on-the-fly activities are the ones most likely to become family traditions.

14. Fast Fun for Daughters Years Four to Seven

Four to Seven / Solo

During these years it's especially important for a dad to establish a tradition of physical activity with his daughter and/or stepdaughter. Girls this age can easily feel very confident in their bodies—a trait you'll want to nurture all the days of her life. So get active with her in ways big and small.

The following suggestions are only starters. You have a lot more ideas inside you—so loosen up, be creative, and have fun together!

Bounce a ball back and forth.
Race each other around the house or the yard.
Climb the jungle gym.
Make up silly words.
Blow bubbles.
Play with the garden hose.
Climb a short tree.
Sing funny songs.
Visit an indoor pool for a swim.
Make things out of cardboard boxes.
Draw or paint pictures.
Play hide-and-seek.
Go swinging together.
Build sand castles at the beach.
Read story or picture books to each other.
Play "go to work."
Make a book that tells a story with pictures.
Bounce on a trampoline.

Tip: Older girls who are physically active are less likely to get into trouble than less active girls. And the most physically active teen girls say that Dad or Stepdad was the one who got them interested in sports and physical activity when they were younger. A great way to use your influence for a good end!

The first thing I notice about a person is _____.

I say that because...

© 2004 Mindamics

15. The Dictionary Game
Six to Eighteen / Group

For generations, families and friends have played The Dictionary Game (aka "Fictionary"). It's one of those activities my grandparents, great-aunts, and great-uncles used to call "parlor games." The object is to trick the other players, use your imagination, and learn new words (but don't tell the kids this last one).

The Dictionary Game requires at least four people—more is better. And everyone has to know how to read and write. All you need is one dictionary and pens and paper for each player.

Start by naming the youngest player as "reader." The reader opens the dictionary randomly and has one minute to pick a word on that page. The more unusual and unknown the word is, the better.

The reader says the word aloud and spells it while the other players write down the word. However, she does NOT give the definition or any hints about what the word actually means.

The other players now have one minute to secretly write down either:

- What they think (or know) the word actually means.
- A funny (but convincing) made-up definition.
- A serious (but convincing) made-up definition.

Meanwhile, the reader writes down the real dictionary definition.

When the minute is up, everyone folds up their paper and hands it to the reader. The reader shuffles them all up and then reads aloud each submitted definition (including the real one). The game works best when the reader is deadpan while reading the submissions, so that no one gets a clue as to the real meaning.

Each player (except for the reader) then votes for what they think the real definition is. (Another strategy is to vote for your own made-up definition, if it appears that other people think yours is the right answer.)

After the voting, the reader reveals the dictionary's definition of the word.

Participants earn points in one of three ways:

- A player earns one point if she/he votes for the correct dictionary definition.
- A player gets one point for every vote other players give to her/his made-up definition.
- The reader gets two points if no one guesses the correct definition.

Moving clockwise, a new person becomes the reader after each round of guessing. You can play up to any number of total points, but we like playing to 21.

Here's an example from a Dictionary Game round I might play with my daughters and some friends. I am the reader, and the dictionary opens to the "O's" and so I choose the word "opsonify." The "definitions" submitted by the players might be as follows:

Nia: business jargon for putting into practice a strategic operations plan.

Sarah: when a father compares the characteristics of two of his sons; one son and then his opposite.

Robert: one of the steps in optical laser correction surgery.

Mavis: what happens to food in the latest, most powerful microwaves—it gets opsonified.

Nancy: to make minute corrections in the balance of audio signals in a recording studio.

The real dictionary definition is "to make [bacteria] more susceptible to destruction by phagocytes by the action of opsonins." (I'll leave it to you to look up what the heck phagocytes and opsonins are!)

In my imaginary game, everyone thought the bacterial definition was fictional. Therefore, no one voted for it—giving me two points (to reward how good my poker face was). Among the other five players, let's say Nia's "definition" got three votes and Nancy's got two votes. That means Nia gets three points, and Nancy two points. The other three players get nothing.

For a different kind of dictionary game, check out the online "Beat the Dictionary" game from Random House at www.randomhouse.com/features/rhwebsters/game.html. It has elements of *Wheel of Fortune,* and you basically race the computer to spell out the word after reading its definition. It works well for kids age ten and up—and even some adults!

Tip: I always liked using quirky words and phrases like "parlor game" with my daughters. I figured it connected them with older family generations they never knew, gave them an expanded (if eccentric) vocabulary, and cemented their view of me as idiosyncratic. Daughters need to experience dads and stepdads as quirky (and even downright odd) because that shows our flexibility, creativity, vulnerability, and ability to enjoy ourselves. Plus, it helps daughters know that they, too, can think and be outside the box when they need to be—or just for fun!

16. Gross-Out Dinner Night

Six to Twelve / Solo and Group

When Jan went off on a birthday trip with friends, her husband Scott and their three daughters planned their first-ever dinner without Mom as "gross-out night" at their North Carolina dinner table. Scott and the girls discovered this method for making fun of the idea that fathers can't handle cooking, housework, or parenting.

We recommend a Gross-Out Dinner as a onetime (or very occasional) activity, a good family Halloween party theme, or a wildly funny activity for a group of fathers and daughters.

Here are the rules (feel free to adjust or re-create to meet your tolerance level):

1. All the food served must look weird and/or have the potential to be messy.
2. No one can use utensils.
3. Eat with your hands (bibs are allowed).
4. No food-throwing.

Recommended menu items:

Mashed potatoes with green food coloring added

Lemonade with brown food coloring added

Meat loaf with lots of ketchup (try eating it without using your hands!)

Macaroni and cheese—the boxed mix kind, not homemade (try eating it without using your hands!)

Green beans, cut in lengths of three inches or more . . . eaten with your toes!

Bread and room-temperature butter or butter substitute in a tub.
   Spread the butter onto the bread with your fingers!

Optional rules:

Burp.
Chew with your mouth open.
Mix different foods together in gross glumps.

For dessert, experienced Gross-Out Dinner chefs recommend Kitty Litter Cake, courtesy of Kelly Land of ParentingHumor.com. (It's not made from kitty litter—it just looks like it is.)

Despite its appearance, the cake is really delicious. For the proper presentation, use a brand new (and definitely unused) plastic cat litter box and spoon it onto plates with a new (NEVER used) pooper scooper.

Ingredients
1 spice or German chocolate cake mix
1 white cake mix
2 large packages vanilla instant pudding mix, prepared
1 large package vanilla sandwich cookies
Green food coloring
12 small Tootsie Rolls
1 NEW kitty litter pan
1 NEW plastic kitty litter pan liner (or waxed paper)
1 NEW pooper scooper (for serving)

Directions
• Prepare cake mixes and bake according to directions (any size pans).
• Prepare pudding mix and chill until ready to assemble.
• Crumble white sandwich cookies in small batches in food processor, scraping often. Set aside all but about 1/4 cup. To the 1/4 cup of cookie crumbs, add a few drops green food coloring and mix until completely colored.

• When cakes are cooled to room temperature, crumble them into a large bowl. Toss the crumbled cake with half of the uncolored white cookie crumbs and the chilled pudding. Important: Mix in just enough of the pudding to moisten it. You don't want it too soggy! Combine gently.

• Line a new, clean kitty litter box with waxed paper. Put the cake/pudding/cookie mixture into the litter box.

• Put 3 unwrapped Tootsie Rolls in a microwave safe dish and heat until they are soft and pliable. Shape the ends so they are no longer blunt, curving slightly. Repeat with 3 more Tootsie Rolls. Bury all 6 in the mixture.

• Sprinkle the other half of the cookie crumbs over the top. Scatter the green cookie crumbs lightly on top of everything—this is supposed to look like the chlorophyll in kitty litter. Heat 3 Tootsie Rolls in the microwave until almost melted. Scrape them on top of the cake; sprinkle with cookie crumbs. Spread remaining Tootsie Rolls over the top; take one and heat until pliable, hang it over the side of the kitty litter box, sprinkling it lightly with cookie crumbs.

• Place the box on a piece of newspaper before serving, and sprinkle a few of the cookie crumbs around for a truly disgusting effect!

• Serve with the brand-new pooper scooper (I know this violates the Gross-Out Dinner's no utensils rule, but it's worth it for the effect).

• You can see a photo of the finished result at:
www.fabulousfoods.com/recipes/dessert/cakes/kittylittercake.html

If you're not a cake fan, you can substitute these yummy gross-out items for dessert: **Brain-shaped gelatin dessert:** The recipe and a way to buy a "brain mold" are available at www.fabulousfoods.com/holidays/halloween/gelatinbrains.html

Halloween worms: There's a recipe at http://www.parentinghumor.com/activityecenter/cookingkids/halloweenworms.htm

Creep me out, man!

Tip: Gross-out and goofy dinners with Dad can be lots of fun. But remember that regular cooking and meal prep is a great way to build closeness with your daughter and take a burden off of your parenting partner(s). Besides, we dads have to stick up for each other and blast away at the moldy old stereotype that the only time dads should be in the kitchen is to perform high farce!

The most beautiful thing in the world is _____.

I say that because...

© 2004 Mindamics

Z
4

17. *The Year-End Collage*

Six to Eighteen / Solo

Many families send annual holiday or year-end letters to update friends and family about important events of the previous twelve months. (Our family, aka "The Procrastinators," usually turns out such letters no earlier than February and no later than June—of the following year.)

The Year-End Collage is a more personal and creative variation on the family holiday letter. It gets you and your daughter to review, remember, and document highlights (and, if you're brave, some lowlights) of your relationship over the previous year. With today's rapidly expanding technology, you can choose other formats besides the collage tradition of pasting cut-up pictures, fancy lettering, and other artwork on a large piece of cardboard to display proudly.

You can also create a website ("LaToya and Her Dad Survive 2008"), write a booklet, make a mix CD or podcast, write a song together, videotape a dramatization—the possibilities keep expanding.

No matter how you do it, make sure the elements you use are directly tied to your own lives and relationship. Some excellent building blocks are:

- Photographs
- Poems
- Letters
- Drawings
- Recordings
- Reflections
- Tickets, programs, or other souvenirs of special events

Creating the Year-End Collage together provides time for the two of you to reflect on what you've done and been through together, what you've learned from and about each other, and how special it is to have a daughter or stepdaughter.

If you do the Year-End Collage *every* December, you'll also have delightful documentation of how she (and perhaps you) have grown up over the years. So whether you're using scissors and glue or HTML, have fun documenting your unique dad-and-daughter adventure.

18. Code Talkers (Or, We've Got a Secret!)

Six to Fourteen / Solo

Everyone loves a secret, and your daughter is no exception. So it's fun to share messages, stories, and laughs in a language that will have the rest of the world wondering what you're talking about. Plus, creating a language that only the two of you speak could be just the thing to keep her talking.

The Joke's on Us

An easy way to start is to make your own inside jokes about people and places you both know. Make references to music, movies, literature, or just be silly. If the local park smells funny because of the swamp behind the baseball field, call it Camp Swampy or Smellington Park. When my daughters complained about being hungry, we'd often offer suggestions such as "Have a peanut butter sandwich." If they complained that they didn't want peanut butter, Nancy or I would say, "I can't read your minds. We're not running the ESP Café."

Soon, all of our family and best friends were referring to our kitchen as "the ESP Café."

Some of the names you dream up will provoke groans (from each other and other people), but even some of those will stick, and her giggles will be a reward for all those eye-rolls when you ask her if she needs more goop for her Meatloaf from the Black Lagoon (Mom's meatloaf with A1 sauce, of course).

Code Fun

Younger girls might have fun talking to you in a code language, like pig latin or gibberish. Both operate by adding a nonsense syllable after each consonant in a word.

The key to gibberish and pig latin is sound addition. Let's say we used a form of gibberish that relies on the sound *idiga*. This is what you use to make normal words sound like gibberish.

Start with a one-syllable word, such as "dog." Take the first letter, in this case "d," and put *idiga* after it so now it sounds like "didiga." Then take the rest of the syllable (not the whole word but just the syllable) and put it after the idiga. So the complete word you would have is didigaog. So "dog" becomes "didigaog."

Now take a two-syllable word, like "flower." Divide it into two syllables: flow-er. Then do the same thing to both syllables as you did for the one syllable word. In this case it would be "flidigowidiger."

Move up to a three-syllable word, such as "beautiful." In gibberish, it's "bidigue-tidigal-fidigal."

For words that start with vowels: A becomes "adiga," E becomes "edige," I is "idigi," and U is "udigu"—so, "animal" would be "adiga-nidigi-midigal." Whew, that's hard to say! (See more at the How to Speak Gibberish website: http://wiki.ehow.com/Speak-Gibberish.)

Pig latin follows slightly different rules for playing with a syllable. The difference is in the nonsense!

When a word begins with a single consonant, move the consonant from the front of the word to the end of the word. Then add "ay" after the consonant. For example, cat becomes "atcay" and mouse becomes "ousemay." The pattern is the same if the word starts with a combined consonant sound; for example, cheese becomes "eesechay."

For words that begin with a vowel, just add yay at the end. For example, is translates as "isyay" and eat as "eatyay."

You can use one of these classics, or invent your own: a language with the first and last syllables flipped, or some sound other than "ay" or "idiga" added after each consonant. For example, "ooga" might better reflect your personal style. "Dog" could become "dooga-googa."

Whatever you two come up with, write out the rules together and practice by speaking your personal language to each other. If you have problems understanding each other, talk about what makes it hard to translate into or out of the language, and how you might fix it—maybe it's hard to speak quickly when you have to make animal sounds instead of the letter "S," or maybe turning all the vowels into "A" is too confusing to understand. Give the language a name and you're good to go.

Codebook

A written code is also a great way to communicate with each other in your own special, secret way. (You might use this sometimes in your DDPJ, on page 24.) Pick an interesting way to change the letters in words. One old standard method is to substitute "z" for "a," "b" for "y," "c" for "x" and so on, continuing to swap early alphabet letters for their later counterparts. You can also turn "a" into "1," "b" into "2"—all the way up to "z" equaling "26."

Actual Letter	A	B	C	D	E	F	G	H	I	J	K	L	M
Number Code	1	2	3	4	5	6	7	8	9	10	11	12	13
Letter Code	z	y	x	w	v	u	t	s	r	q	p	o	n

Actual Letter	N	O	P	Q	R	S	T	U	V	W	X	Y	Z
Number Code	14	15	16	17	18	19	20	21	22	23	24	25	26
Letter Code	m	l	k	j	i	h	g	f	e	d	c	b	a

Use the number code from the chart above, and "I want grilled cheese" would read: 9 23.1.14.20 7.18.9.12.12.5.4 3.8.5.5.19.5.

Using the letter code, "I want grilled cheese" would read: R dzmg tiroovw xsvvhv.

Then there are codes a cryptographer might relish, like making a new symbol for each letter or developing a way that "a" could mean anything from itself to "z"—depending if it's written on line 1 or line 26. Make a codebook so you'll be able to translate each other's notes. You might want to keep especially meaningful notes in English, since you could forget or lose the key to a complicated code. (It makes my head hurt just thinking about it!)

New Language Frontiers

If you're a more ambitious father-daughter pair, you could create—or at least plan—a complete new language. To keep it simple, use patterns often, limit the vocabulary to everyday items, and try to relate the words of your language to English words: a car could be a "drive-a-dim," a chair a "sit-a-sim," eating "meal-ska," practicing for music lessons "piano-ska."

Find new endings for nouns and verbs, writing it all down as you go—it might seem obvious as you create your language that Mom is called "Pompom," but in a few days it could easily be forgotten. Even if you don't become fluent in your language, mixing some of it into everyday speech will be enough to confound your audience. Telling your daughter "Let's car-ska to the buy-shoes-a-bim" and hearing her respond "Can we stop at the ice cream place for some yum-eat-a-yim on the way home?" is guaranteed to confuse and perplex—and leave a smile on your face.

Saying "I Love You"

These three magic words help hold a family together, but they can be very hard to say. Teenage daughters especially tend to resist this most basic show of affection, even to the point of objecting when you say it to them.

One simple solution: Make a sign, symbol, or code word to stand for "I love you," so she won't be embarrassed or angry, but you can still express your feelings for each other. Use a rhyming word, a common expression with a twist—"heavens above!"—or a special gesture, like holding up three fingers or putting your hand to your heart.

In American Sign Language, you tell your daughter "I love you" by pointing at yourself, then crossing your wrists across your heart, then pointing at your daughter. Or, you can hold your hand up, palm out, with pinky, thumb, and index finger up, while the middle and ring finger are folded down (like you'd have them in a fist). That single gesture is an ASL "shorthand" for I Love You.

Any one of these "alternative" methods of communication allow you to show how much you care about her (even in public) without upsetting her. That's especially important when she gets older, as she may become easily embarrassed by your public shows of affection. But if you two start developing special, fun, and/or nonverbal ways of saying "I love you" when she is young, those unique symbols can be a safe and secret code for you both during her adolescence—and beyond.

Daughters who are more comfortable with you saying "I love you" might appreciate a new twist to make them feel good when they least expect it. Write those three important words on a note slipped into her backpack, in icing on a cupcake, or in the middle of a list of chores. Knowing that Dad loves you and is thinking of you, even when he's not around, is very reassuring for a daughter.

Just remember what the gibberish expert tells his daughter every day: "Idigi Lidigove Udigu!"

> **Tip:** Another fun way to invent your own "code" is to learn a second language that already exists. Take lessons together in Spanish, Swahili, Mandarin, French, Japanese, Russian, Norwegian—the list goes on and on.

19. *Hina Matsuri (Girls' Day)*

Six to Fourteen / Solo and Group

Every March 3, Japanese families celebrate a holiday called Hina Matsuri—Girls' Day. There is no analogous national holiday in North America, but you and your daughter can create a Girls' Day in your own family or community.

Hina Matsuri began as a Shinto holy day of purification, similar to the most sacred Jewish holy day, Yom Kippur. Shinto worshippers created paper dolls to represent their impurities, and then put the dolls in a river to wash away their shortcomings. In recent centuries the holiday has evolved into a ritual display of fancy dolls during a day on which families celebrate their daughters and pray for their girls' future health and success.

According to the University of Florida's Dr. Judy Shoaf (a collector of Japanese dolls), girls and their parents (usually mothers) take the dolls—called *hina*—out of storage and display them on a fancy, draped structure, like a small altar. The most exalted pair of dolls stands on the highest level, while below, "lesser" dolls pretend to serve them sake, play music, or guard the "royal" couple from intruders.

As part of the celebration, girls host their friends for a party and pretend to serve food to the dolls using tiny dish sets. The festival's name, Hina Matsuri, combines the word for dolls *(hina)* and the word for festival *(matsuri)*.

To create your own version of Hina Matsuri, think about what you and your daughter want to celebrate about girls, what it means to be a girl, and the unique girl your daughter is. Those qualities might include:

Honesty
Courage
Caring

Love of animals
Curiosity
Keen analytical skills
Artistic talent

You and your daughter can adapt the Japanese custom by making a display of dolls and/or stuffed animals that portray special qualities about her. Alternately, you can create works of art, writing, music, or performance as well.

Be creative about what you want to celebrate on your Girls' Day and how you want to celebrate it. You can also broaden the celebration to include other girls in your family (sisters, moms, aunts, grandmothers, cousins).

A Girls' Day is a great activity to do with other father-daughter pairs in your neighborhood or your daughter's school. The enthusiasm generated may snowball into a community-wide Girls' Day celebration. And then, who knows, maybe we'll start such a big trend that our entire country will declare an official Girls' Day, just like in Japan!

Tip: Send photos, artwork, and stories about your unique Girls' Day celebration to Dads & Daughters at the *Dads & Daughters Togetherness Guide* website (see p. 168). We're putting the best examples up on the website and highlighting them in our online e-newsletter.

20. *Those Yarn Dolls*

Six to Nine / Solo and Group

You can buy your daughter hundreds of different kinds of dolls, from Bratz (gag me) to American Girl to precious porcelain collectibles. But based on the same experience that shows kids often enjoying the cardboard box that held the toy more than the toy itself, try creating a homemade doll and see what she does with it.

The simplest kind of homemade doll is made of yarn. You'll need the following materials:

> Yarn (duh!)
> A Ping-Pong ball
> Scissors
> Sewing needle and thread
> Buttons
> Scraps of fabric

Start by cutting between 20 and 25 one-foot lengths of yarn (the thicker the yarn, the fewer pieces you'll need). Lay them down in one even bunch. Then take a small piece of yarn and tie all the pieces together just down from the top—it will look something like the top of an old-fashioned haystack. (Figure 1)

Next, insert the Ping-Pong ball right below the spot you tied off, and surround it with the yarn. You can substitute a wad of cotton or bunched-up fabric if you don't have a Pong-Pong ball—but don't

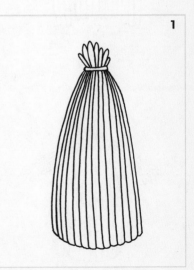

1

choose something too hard, like a rock or golf ball. (Figure 2) Then, use another small piece of yarn to tie together the bunch of yarn just below the Ping-Pong ball. Voilà, you have the doll's head. (Figure 3)

Now, pull away five to seven pieces of yarn from each side of the bunch to make arms. Tie the arms off about four inches down, and cut off the excess below the knot. Your arms are done. (Figure 4)

Tie another small piece of yarn around the remaining center bunch to create the waist. (Figure 5)

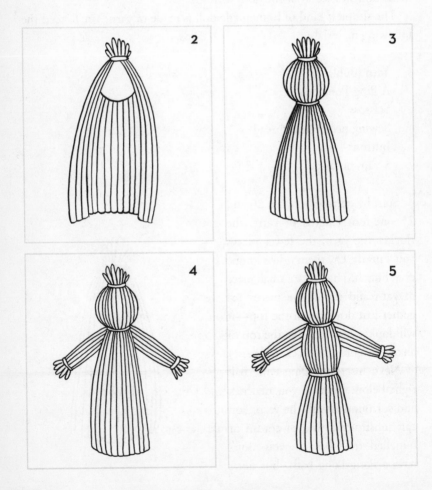

Below the waist, split the yarn in half, and tie off both ends to make the two legs. (Figure 6)

Finally, sew buttons on the head to make eyes, and a piece of fabric to make a mouth. You can also drape and/or sew other pieces of fabric to make clothing, depending on how elaborate you want to be. (Figures 7, 8)

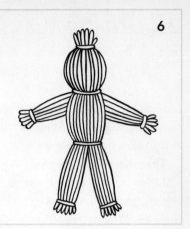

These instructions may read as more daunting than the actual doll construction is in practice. Once you do a couple, the two of you can whip off dozens of Those Yarn Dolls in no time. Then she'll have a collection of dolls that sprang from her own hands!

Tip: Remember that stepfathers and fathers have a very important role when it comes to their daughters' dolls. That role is to play dolls with those daughters—it's the manly thing to do!

21. *Driving Miss Daughter*
Eight to Fifteen / Solo

One of the simplest activities you can do with your daughter is something you might be doing already, or else something that may be very easy to start doing right away:

Drive her where she needs to go.

Drive her to school, sports practice, dance class, play rehearsal, church, martial arts class, visual arts class, manual arts class . . . you get the idea. Driving your daughter or stepdaughter places provides a predictable and safe way to talk with and listen to each other.

Think about it: When you're in the car, you are together in a small room. It's very unlikely either one of you will leave the room until you get to your destination—it really messes up your clothes to jump out while the car is still moving.

To make a run-of-the-mill car ride into a Driving Miss Daughter experience, follow these four simple rules (which apply to both dad and daughter):

1. All audio/video equipment is turned off (including cell phones and iPods), and ears are free of headphones
2. No lecturing
3. Dad listens more than he talks
4. No jumping out of the car if it is still in motion

When my daughters were grade-school age, I worked as the morning news anchor at a radio station; I went to work by 4:00 A.M. and was home most days by early afternoon. That meant I got to drive the girls to ballet class, tae kwon do, music lessons, and other places almost every day.

Not every car ride led to profound conversations. Most days I enforced only rule number 4. (Well, to tell the truth, I never had to enforce rule number 4—my kids figured that one out on their own.) But at least once a week I'd keep the radio off and we'd talk to each other, with me trying my best to be the primary listener.

Whenever I was a carpool driver, I always kept the radio off. That's so I could eavesdrop on the conversations my daughters and their friends were having. This is the big carpooling secret that only experienced parents know—if the parent stays quiet, the kids soon forget that he is there, and they start revealing things the parent might never discover on his own.

If we fathers and stepfathers stop and reflect for a moment, it quickly becomes clear that a daughter's childhood is so fascinating, we seldom lack for motivation to be part of it. Of course, we have to take the simple step of making time in our lives for this special relationship—even if it's just volunteering to be the driver more often. Then, we have to keep our eyes and ears open if we hope to figure out who she is and what comes next.

A dad gains many benefits from Driving Miss Daughter, but he can't get them unless his butt is in the driver's seat. So if your schedule allows it, drive her someplace she needs to go, and do it at least once a week. If she takes the bus to school, arrange to drive her instead every Wednesday. That car ride becomes your special time together—when you can dedicate your attention to her (and the road) and show her how important she is to you.

22. *Get Lost!*

Ten to Fifteen / Solo

This is a variation on the more utilitarian task of driving your daughter around to her various activities. Life for kids and adults nowadays is very scheduled, chop-chop, and fast-paced. This very simple activity can slow you both down so you can wander along without any agenda, or any need to accomplish a thing—except hang out together.

Get in the car and drive for some short period of time (say 20 to 30 minutes), with no particular destination. You and your daughter can take turns deciding which way to turn and when—but, whenever possible, turn onto roads you've never traveled before.

You can also try having her direct you to a place of her choosing while you try to guess where she is leading you. Or you can tell her where you want to go to see if she can direct you. This builds navigation and communication skills.

While you're lost, keep an eye out for interesting sites or activities you can stop to look at—or even join in!

- Maybe you'll find a fruit stand you never knew was there; get out and ask the farmer to talk about this year's crop.
- Maybe you'll find a hole-in-the-wall hardware store you'd never heard of; park and poke around for hidden treasures.
- Maybe you'll spy a pickup softball game going on in a city park; go over and ask if you can play a couple of innings.
- Maybe you'll find a new neighborhood where you can try to drive or walk down every street in the neighborhood.

My friend Bob Stien lives outside New York City. He's a divorced dad, so when his daughters were young, he liked to make use of every minute of their visits to his house.

We called it "the Navigator Game." When I had a half hour before I had to return them to their mom's home, I would give each child ten minutes to direct me where to drive the car. "Turn right here, Dad . . . then left at that big tree. . . ." After they'd each had their ten minutes playing navigator, I'd start figuring out where we were and how to get back. It was a fun challenge!

Over the years, we stopped to listen to a man play bagpipes, stopped to watch a bunny work its way across a field, and many other "small" things that ended up creating big memories.

You can also drive someplace more intentional. Plan a road trip together with your daughter, plotting out the route on a map, researching interesting places to visit along the way, scheduling time to see those interesting places—and the amazing things that just pop up as you drive along.

For example, I recently drove to Dubuque, Iowa. The route took me through Dyersville, where the movie *Field of Dreams* was filmed. Being a big baseball fan, I had to stop. It was then I discovered that Dyersville is also home to numerous factories (with outlet stores!) that make miniature toy vehicles and farm equipment. It was a blast!

23. *Papa Poetry*
Eight to Eighteen / Solo

Not sure if you're a poet? Well, like most other things in life, it depends on how you define it. Here are a couple of ways to create fun and memorable verse together. Come up with your own ideas, and remember:

- Poetry doesn't always have to rhyme!
- Save what you write, because you'll both cherish it later.

Acronym Art

Acronyms are words formed from the first letters or syllables of other words. It's fun and fairly easy to turn one another's names (or a word you both love) into an acronym—which is a kind of poetry! I'll use my daughters' names to demonstrate two examples of acronym poetry: one that describes some of Nia's qualities, and another that tells about something Mavis did (during a weaving class).

Nurturing
Intense
Amazing

Multicolors
Attached
Vivid
Incandescent
Secret

An acronym poem can have one or more words to a line. If you have two or more words per line, you can try to make every word on the line begin with the same letter—or just make the first word of each line correspond to the acronym you're working from. For example, here's one I wrote about Nia dancing a lead role in the local ballet company's *Nut-cracker.*

> Nervous, she tames every energy with her breath
> Immediately on cue, leaps smoothly on stage, strong and
> Aglow with character, confidence and joy.

Start by making acronym poetry out of each other's names. If she wants more than the three letters of D-A-D to work with, let her use your given name. (If your name is Sy or Pat, tell her "tough luck!") You can also use other words—like your favorite vacation spot. One more reason to visit Ontonagon and Kaunakakai!

Couples Composition

You can make "tag-team" poetry, taking turns writing a line or stanza of verse. You can do it in the style of the old "telephone" game—just start writing and see what fun places it takes you, or agree on your subject matter before you start. Here's one about a daughter's rite of passage.

> Daughter: The first day I dyed my hair,
> Dad: I thought, "She wouldn't dare!"
> Daughter: I wasn't sure I wanted you there.
> Dad: But I wanted to show I care.
> Daughter: So, you came and pulled up a chair.
> Dad: And you went about it with such flair!
> Daughter: On the day when I first dyed my hair.

Of course, rhyming poetry is sometimes harder to write than free verse. For a real challenge, work to get each of your lines in the same meter and rhyming pattern. Sometimes the discipline of following "traditional" structure (like a sonnet form) can push you two to new heights of creativity, and other times it might get in the way. Do what works best for both of you.

For help with rhyming, check out Rhyme Zone at www.rhyme zone.com.

Solo Sonnetry

Another way to write poetry together is for you to work independently of each other, while addressing the same subject. Here's a poem called "The Wonder Kid" where Pere Robert uses traditional rhyming patterns and humor to share an important insight. (But don't rule out free verse and serious approaches, either!)

The Wonder Kid
—by Pere Robert

It's tough sometimes to be a dad,
Especially when your kid is bad.
You wonder why she did what she did
—And why she's not a wonder kid.

A wonder kid is always good.
A wonder kid does what she should.
A wonder kid is never bad.
A wonder kid makes daddies glad.

She doesn't shout, she doesn't fight,
She goes to bed on time each night.
She makes her bed, she eats her peas,
She always says, "yes, sir" and "please."

She never whines and never mopes.
She likes to bathe, and uses soap.
She chews her food, she doesn't slurp,
And when she's through she doesn't burp.

She wears her mittens when it freezes.
She's kind to pets and never teases.
She cares for toys and likes to share them.
Her clothes get cleaner as she wears them.

"Did you ever hear of such a kid?"
I asked my kid, who never did.
And then, oh boy, was I surprised
When my little girl apologized:

"I'm sorry for the thing I did.
I wish I were a wonder kid.
I wish that I could make you glad.
I love you so, my wonder Dad."

I hemmed and hawed, I coughed and sputtered,
The butterflies in my stomach fluttered.
I'd focused on her faults, but she
Had only seen the good in me.

It's tough sometimes to be a kid,
Especially when Dad blows his lid.
You wonder how he gets that way,
And why he takes so long to say:

"I love you too, I'm really glad
To know you think I'm a wonder dad,
And I wouldn't change you, not a bit—
You already are a wonder kid."

(Copyright Pere Robert and reprinted with permission of the author.)

Imagine the verse this poet's daughters might have written to describe their frustrations and insights about him.

Writing poetry together (or individually about each other) lets you go in any direction you can imagine. Reach into nature, history (personal or otherwise), your imagination, or anywhere else for images and ideas to convey your thoughts and feelings.

> **Tip:** Be sure to take any poetry you write together and include it in your Dad and Daughter Private Journal (see p. 24).

Tweens

The preteen and early teen years (labeled the "tweens" by many folks) are the time when a girl's vision and attention start turning outward from herself and family to incorporate more awareness of the larger world, with all of its mysteries, joys, contradictions, confusion, opportunities, barriers, and excitement.

According to research into girls' emotional and psychological development, girls are normally loud, opinionated, and physically confident until age twelve or so. But then a typical girl begins to silence her voice and herself.

The sassy, tree-climbing ten-year-old (with feet spread wide, chest puffed out, and an opinionated answer for every question) assumes she will be taken seriously when she shouts, "That's not fair!" However, this strutting child often turns into a soft-spoken, passive thirteen-year-old (with timid stance, shoulders hunched to hide her chest, and answers of "I don't know" to even the most basic questions) who may still demand justice from the world—but, strangely, not for herself.

Granted, the energy and rough edges of the ten-year-old can be a little tough to live with, but there seem to be few signs in the thirteen-year-old that her younger self ever existed. Where did she go? Underground? Why does she feel the need to silence her voice?

My wife, Nancy Gruver, publisher of the girls' magazine *New Moon*, writes, "A girl silences herself because she encounters a culture that still encourages her, in ways both subtle and blatant, to put her own needs second. A culture that is extraordinarily uncomfortable with girls who know what they want and expect to get it; a culture that labels girls' complaints as whining and their pursuit of their desires as bitchiness and self-centered."

A girl feels good about herself when she is loud and bold. Then she runs into the notion (sometimes reinforced by Dad) that loud behavior is not ladylike. She hears that it's unattractive to recognize your own needs and speak up openly for them. People (sometimes within her family) begin seeing her as a sexual object rather than as a person. She begins to wear the gender straightjacket that rewards her more for her looks, passivity, and being soft-spoken than for her passions, insights, and beliefs.

But Dad holds as much power (and sometimes more) as anyone in a girl's life to help her resist this silencing of who she is.

Active, playful involvement is key. In the introduction we discussed how play fosters openness and authenticity in daughters and fathers. During the "tween" years, girls need to maintain contact with their authentic heart and soul. Play helps her do that, and play with Dad gives her the powerful message that there is always a safe, fun place to be her true self—while enjoying the company of the most influential man in her life: you.

24. Fast Fun for Daughters Years Eight to Ten

Eight to Ten / Solo

By this age, girls are starting to spend more time with school friends. And thus starts the years-long challenge of preserving sacred time for you and your daughter or stepdaughter to spend together, just the two of you. Keep the tradition strong now, and it will be easier to do it later!

The following suggestions are only starters. Use them to come up with more of your own!

Play an instrument.
Read a book together.
Play Crazy Eights, Old Maid, and other card games.
"Paint" temporary pictures on the sidewalk with a big brush and water.
Make a tent out of a sheet over a table.
Go for a walk, a run, or a bike ride.
Look at insects.
Play basketball with a crumpled-up piece of paper and a wastebasket.
Take her to work with you.
Plant a garden.
Go to the park.
Play a board game.
Play house.
Play make-believe (chef, doctor, mechanic, business owner, pilot, astronaut, teacher, etc.).
Practice whistling.
Collect baseball cards.
Ride a bike trail together.
Rebound while she shoots hoops.
Thumb wrestle.
Play paper football.

25. *Your Day in History*

Ten to Fourteen / Solo

Every one of us has a birthday, and there are thousands of famous and influential people in history. That means that you and your daughter share birthdays with several people of note.

For example, in one quick web search, I found that I share my birthday with Petula Clark, Sam Waterston, William Pitt the Elder, Gen. Erwin Rommel, Georgia O'Keeffe, Mantovani, and Anni-Frid Lyngstad (aka Fryeda Anderson of the rock group Abba). Or they share theirs with me, depending on how you look at it. I also found that actor Beverly D'Angelo (*National Lampoon Vacation* movies) and I were born on exactly the same date. Even so, we've never met—probably because we don't run in the same circle.

I also discovered that the following people died on my birth date: seventeenth-century German astronomer Johannes Kepler, actor Tyrone Power, and anthropologist Margaret Mead.

Look up your daughter's birthday, and then look up your own. You can write down what you find in your DDPJ. You both might even find a particularly interesting bit of historical trivia associated with her or your birthday that you don't tell anyone else, so it remains your own special secret.

You can make this an ongoing project as you continue to search out notable events in world history, movies, sports, and other areas. You might go back to newspapers published on each one of your birthdays through the years, and then list the notable headlines—a project you could keep doing for the rest of your life.

In addition to knowing who was born and died on your birthday, you can investigate what important historical events happened on the day you were born, and on your birth date in other years. On my birthday in 1777, the Articles of Confederation were adopted by the newly formed United States; in 1956, Elvis Presley's first film was released; and in 1977, the 100 millionth Ford was built.

Here is a potpourri of Internet sites that can connect you to most dates in the year—and tickle your interest on any day of the year (these sites were up and running at the time this book was being written):

- Uncle Woody's Almanac—www.unclewoody.org. My favorite; a fabulous, easy-to-use reference for every date in the year.
- Anyday Today in History—www.scopesys.com/anyday/.
- My Virtual Reference Desk Daily Almanac—www.refdesk.com/quote.html. Lets you know what's happening today.
- This Day in North American Indian History—http://americanindian.net/#Dates. A little clunky to use, but lots of information.
- Bizarre American Holidays—http://library.thinkquest.org/2886/. A database of strange things to celebrate.
- Black Facts Online—www.blackfacts.com. Find out things that happened on any day in Black History.
- Daily Miscellany—www.geocities.com/Athens/Forum/1327/old _dm.html. History, birthdays, and events.
- dMarie Time Capsule—www.dmarie.com/timecap/. Allows you to find headlines, popular music and TV shows, birthdays, and more for the date you pick.
- The Internet Movie Database—www.imdb.com/M/on-this-day. On this day in movie history.
- The History Channel: This Day In History—www.historychannel .com/tdih/tdih.jsp?category=leadstory. Easy to use and lots of variety.
- eLibrary's Today's Birthdays: www.elib.com/Calendar/Events/birthday.php. Allows you to choose any date.
- Today in Radical History—www.he.net/cgi-bin/suid/~radtours/today.cgi. Learn about historic radical events for any date.

Tip: For my money, the most interesting type of person is a reference librarian. So head down to your local public library and introduce yourself. Reference librarians can hook you up with almanacs, encyclopedias, and other great resources to do your research. Many of them can also steer you to great online reference sources. Be sure to say "Hi!" from me.

26. *Home Inventing*
Ten to Eighteen / Solo

Do you and your daughter ever notice things around the house that you wish were more efficient? Do you ever think there ought to be an invention to solve a seemingly unsolvable problem? Do you ever wish there was a product to help you do something better?

Try doing some home invention brainstorming and innovating. You could try to solve one of my pet peeves: how to get flour from the bag into the mixing bowl without having some of it spill and blow all over the kitchen counter. Plus, cleaning it up makes the dishrag all goopy!

Everyday annoyances often lead to great innovations. For example, the Norwegian patent office reports that the cheese-slicer was invented by Lillehammer carpenter Thor Bjørklund in 1927. He wanted thinner slices of gouda in his sandwiches, and a knife didn't work the way he wanted.

Experimenting with his tools, Thor found that a wood plane worked pretty well, but was too big and impractical to store in a kitchen. After thinking about the problem overnight, he cut a thin slice of steel, bending a small part down, while the back of the steel-slice was bent up so a nice slice of cheese would go through. Neighbors and friends loved his invention, word spread, he had a new business—and eventually he also had Norway's patent number 43377.

The key is to think wildly and dream big (or small, if the problem is tiny). Don't let "practicality" get in the way.

When inventing, guessing is right; even if it doesn't immediately lead to an answer. Remember that Thomas Edison tried hundreds of variations before finding the right filament for a light bulb that could be mass-produced.

The Girls Scouts of the USA recommend three important things to keep in mind when working with a girl on projects:

- Let her take the lead in handling materials, giving directions, and exploring.

- Work as a team—don't set out to compete.
- Give her time to think and explore. Silence often means that thinking is going on (get more fatherly tips at www.girlsgotech .org/girlsgotech_booklet.pdf).

There are numerous websites aimed at encouraging girls to be inventive and enthusiastic about science and technology. Here are just a few:

- Inventive Kids (www.inventivekids.com)
- Girl Tech (www.girltech.com)
- Girls Go Tech, from the Girl Scouts of the USA (www.girls gotech.org)
- The U.S. Patent and Trademark Office Kids Pages (www.uspto .gov/go/kids)
- By Kids For Kids (www.bkfk.com)
- FIRST: For Inspiration and Recognition of Science and Technology (www.usfirst.org)
- The National Inventor's Hall of Fame in Akron has a summer program for kids in grades one through six called Camp Invention (www.invent.org/camp_invention/)

A visit to Patently Absurd (http://totallyabsurd.com/) will treat you to many attempts to solve everyday problems, like the wet diaper alarm, all-terrain stroller, and baby cage. Things get even wilder when you look beyond toddlerhood.

Tip: Keep in mind that inventing doesn't have to mean creating a whole new technology. For example, you and your daughter can invent a new way to paint or wallpaper her bedroom. Or even your bedroom! Maintain a broad definition of inventing, and there will be more room for both of you to move around and have fun.

27. Family Treasure Chest
Ten to Eighteen / Solo

You know that you and your daughter are the product of a long family lineage and history. Did you also know how enjoyable and useful that history can be to both of you right now?

My grandfather traveled to Europe occasionally for work, and once brought home a 35mm Zeiss camera, which became central to his passion for a particular kind of photography: taking slides of his family. I eventually inherited many boxes of these slides, which include pictures taken before I was born (I have no idea who some of these people are, even though they are apparently relatives). They also include photos of my grade school graduation, and hundreds of images of his grandchildren, nieces, nephews, in-laws, siblings, and dozens of their friends and neighbors.

These photos—and the stories behind them—are a rich treasure trove for my daughters and me. They allow me to tell the girls about their heritage and the amazing women and men who came before them on my side of the family. They provided amusing evenings and great opportunities to instill the things our family has held dear for generations. They are also my latest project—I'm scanning the slides into my computer so that I can share all of the digital photos with my sisters and cousins, and also so I can get my aunt to help me identify those unknown relatives.

Here are two simple ways that you and your daughter can explore and embrace your family history.

When I Was a Boy
Gather together photographs, programs, school essays, and other souvenirs of you and your family from the days of your own childhood. If you don't have them in your possession, ask your parents, siblings, or other relatives for copies.

Tell your daughters stories about your youth, and encourage your daughter to ask you probing questions about what happened, who the various players were (or are), what came before, what came after, and more. Remember to tell stories, not parental lectures or instruction thinly disguised as morality tales. These stories and characters may be vivid or old hat to you, but they are brand-new to her.

Here are a few sample questions to get her started:

- What was the most important event in your life (and why) when you were ten? Fifteen? Twenty?
- Who had had the most positive impact on you by the time you were ten? Fifteen? Twenty?
- What is the funniest thing you ever saw or participated in yourself?
- What do you think is the most important change in the world between the time you were my age and today?
- Which of your own ancestors provided you with your greatest inspiration growing up?

Write down and/or record theses stories—and any interviews or conversations that your daughter has with you about them. Call or write relatives to ask for their memories about these incidents, or for their own memories of growing up with you in your family.

Be open to wherever these questions, conversations, and memories take you and your daughter. They can be a fantastic way for her to get to know you more deeply. Plus, the questions and conversations are bound to get more complex, interesting, and moving as she gets older. Be creative in how you preserve these memories—construct a scrapbook or enter items in your DDPJ (see p. 24).

> **Tip:** In the modern world of computers, it is entirely possible to copy and/or scan items (including old photos and slides) into digital files. This allows other relatives to share old images and mementos with you, and vice versa. Such sharing keeps family history alive for any relative who wants to use it. For example, sending your brother that photo of you two playing ball when you were twelve might spark a wonderful conversation between him and his child.

The Genealogy Gang

The digital world is also sparking a flood of interest in genealogy. Working with your daughter to trace your family roots and uncover stories about your ancestors is great fun and very informative.

These websites offer free (and vast) resources for searching through old records for links to a family's past:

www.familysearch.org
www.genhomepage.com
www.usgenweb.org
www.ancestorhunt.com
(Google "genealogy," and you'll find even more)

You can also tap older living relatives for stories and family history. Doing this with your daughter can open doors and break down resistance from even the most crotchety great aunt. Plus, it will likely introduce you to stories and information you didn't know about before.

Be creative in whatever directions your research and conversations go. This effort can even translate into a school project for your daughter eventually (another incentive for her to participate).

Stories and photographs of your ancestors can be a powerful foundation for your daughter's self-image. In a world that often worships superficial appearance and absurd standards of female "perfection," a sense of connection with ancestors can really help a girl. Here's an example from my book *Dads & Daughters: How to Inspire, Understand, and Support Your Daughter* (Broadway, 2003):

> *When my daughter said she was tired of being teased because she had so many freckles, I said, "Let's get out Grandpa's old slides. Look at all these freckles; everywhere you look, our relatives have freckles. Here's a real strawberry face—your great, great aunt Catherine, who was married less than a year before her husband ran off. Know what she did? Went to work for a big New York restaurant chain and worked her way up to become an executive— quite a feat for a woman in the 1950s!"*

—Matt

In a quick and natural turn of conversation, Matt showed his daughter that freckles are "the way it is" in her clan, that her foremothers were women of accomplishment, and that there are plenty of colorful, fascinating stories in her very own family—stories more interesting than what she'll find in *Seventeen*. He put her in touch with important truths about who she is and from where she comes. These *real* role models make excellent alternatives to the latest pop stars or other celebrities-du-jour.

28. *The Little Rock Exercise*

Six to Sixteen / Solo and Group

I call this the Little Rock Exercise because I first created it for a father-daughter retreat sponsored by Arkansas Children's Hospital. The name still works, though, because those small moments of enjoyment we share with our daughters are the "little rocks" on which we build a strong, loving, and lasting relationship. Plus, those moments are fun!

All you need for this exercise is paper and pencil (or pen). On a separate piece of paper, each participant (one daughter and one father) fills in the blanks and circles their answers. There are no right or wrong answers—the idea is to learn about the other person, and then agree to have fun together. (Photocopying these two pages makes it easy.)

Step One

The last time we [daughter and father] had fun together was when we
_____.

I had a good time because _____.

My (father/daughter) would (agree/disagree) that this was a fun time.

My (father/daughter) and I spend time together doing fun things about ___ times a (week/month/year).

Other (fathers/daughters) probably spend (more/less) time having fun together than we do.

I think my (father/daughter) spends too much time _____ and not enough time _____.

I have the most fun with my (father/daughter) when he/she _____
_____.

One thing that my (father/daughter) enjoys doing is _____
_____.

Two things that I like doing with my (father/daughter) that take at least 30 minutes are _____ and _____.

I would like to spend half a day _____ with my (father/daughter).

Step Two

Daughter and father swap papers with each other and compare and discuss their answers for five to ten minutes.

Step Three

Each participant fills in the following blanks individually:

What my father/daughter wrote confirmed for me that _____

_____.

The thing that took me most by surprise about what he/she wrote was _____.

He/she can't help _____ because _____.

Two concrete things I want to do now are _____ and

_____.

Step Four

As a pair, the father-daughter duo fills in the following blanks and signs off on it.

For at least 30 minutes at a time, we will _____ at least once a week.

We agree to keep up this schedule until _____, at which time we'll review our agreement.

Signatures:

_____

Daughter/Stepdaughter

_____

Father/Stepfather

_____

Date

Tape your agreement to the refrigerator door or another prominent place where both of you will see it daily.

29. The Official List of Very Silly Things

Five to Ten / Solo and Group

When my daughters were young, we loved coming up with lists of very silly things. We did this best when we were already in a goofy or giddy mood, and then launched spontaneously into riffing on some ridiculous and fantastical train of thought.

The key is to relax and be silly. Relaxing and being silly can come a little more naturally for a kid than for a dad, so let go and have fun!

Here's an example of a List of Very Silly Things that my daughter Nia and I created once. Note that the list contains almost entirely foolish, ridiculous, and/or tongue-in-cheek ideas.

Multiple Uses for Pez Dispensers

Hedge clippers
Insect catcher
Embosser
Paper hole puncher
Paper clip dispenser
Stapler
Staple remover
CD holder (single)
Holder of mini holiday lights
Tack dispenser
Clamp
Pliers
Vise-Grips
Dust bunny eater
Button holder
Message holder

Mail/Bill caddy
Picks up lettuce leafs
Toenail clippers\tweezers
Hood ornament
Doorstop
Scrabble tile holder
Baby rattle
Scarecrow
Party place-card holder
Hair clip
Bookend
Page-turner
Picks up dirty socks
Diaper pin
Clothespin
Ear-piercer
Ornament atop a car antenna

Multiple Uses for Pez Candies

Dollhouse dominoes
Jewelry
Mini-mini chess
Pez therapy
Holiday decorations
Food decorations
Flavored Alka-Seltzer
Line driveways and sidewalks
Gingerbread house decorations
Dollhouse bricks
Beads
Plant decorations
Rubber stamps
Pez chip cookies
Pez pancakes

So find an item, event, personality, or anything else around your house and start making your very own Dad & Daughter Official List of Very Silly Things.

Or really cut loose, and make more than one DDOLVST! And don't forget to add your DDOLVST to your DDPJ. Do it ASAP!

30. Can You Shop This?

Six to Twelve / Solo

This is a fun word game that builds memory skills for both you and your daughter. If you're like me, memorizing things can give you a headache. But this game makes memorization fun while generating lots of laughter.

The goal is to compete in memorizing a list of at least twenty-six words. Start by letting your daughter pick any letter in the alphabet, for example, "J". She then has to say out loud an item she could buy which starts with that letter. So, she might say, "I will buy some jelly."

You have to go next. You repeat her choice, and then add another item that starts with the next letter of the alphabet. So, you might say, "I will buy some jelly and some Krispy Kremes."

Now it's her turn again. She must repeat the two choices already spoken, and then add another item beginning with the following letter, "L". So, she might say, "I will buy some jelly, Krispy Kremes, and lard." Then the "shopping list" is passed back to you for repetition and addition of something starting with "M". You get the idea. (Parenthetical funny remarks like "Mmmmm—this list contains a perfectly balanced diet!" are always welcome.)

With each turn, the list gets longer and harder to memorize. But the items you each add to your "shopping list" will probably include some amusing things, and the struggle to remember it all will also add to the laughter.

Keep the competition light, with the focus on fun. For example, don't disqualify someone for saying "x-tra buttons" when you traverse the treacherous territory between "W" and "Y". Encourage silly and fantastical items, like aardvark, brontosaurus, cauldron, and Detroit. To increase the challenge, go two or more rounds through the alphabet without repeating any items on your "shopping" list.

Tip: This is a Potentially Quite Really Super Terrific Unbelievable Vibrant Wonderful X-tremely Yummy Zowie-filled game to play with the whole family, or with a group of fathers and daughters. The more brains in the mix, the wilder it gets.

For a variation, try composing a sentence that uses twenty-six words that start with the letters of the alphabet, in order. Anybody but Charlie does excessive foolishness gracefully, however I just . . .

One thing I did that was "out-of-character" for me was _____.

I say that because...

© 2005 Mindamics

M
14

31. Fast Fun for Daughters Years Eleven to Thirteen

Eleven to Thirteen / Solo

Many people are skeptical that girls this age would want to have anything to do with their stepfathers or fathers. But as long as we make our time together predictable, fun, enthusiastic—and (when necessary) invisible from her friends—she'll find a way to be part of it. So if she starts to resist spending time with you, respect her needs—but keep pushing for your special time together (see "Will This Work?" on p. 5). She needs you to prove your loyalty by sticking with her even during the times she pushes you (temporarily) away.

Here are a few suggestions to get you started. Feel free to add more ideas of your own, and remember that the most important thing is to have fun!

Build a model together.
Tune up your bikes.
Make a birthday card for someone.
Look up words in the dictionary.
Go camping.
Build a fort together.
Tell scary stories.
Tell loving stories.
Talk about what you did as a kid.
Cook a meal together.
Volunteer for the elderly.
Toss a football or baseball.
In-line skate together.
Go bowling.
Bird-watch.
Play four-square.

Draw aliens.

Go shopping with her for a "special occasion" outfit.

Go for a night drive.

Make a night game with flashlights.

Gaze at the sky and describe what animals the clouds look like.

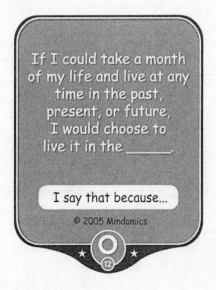

If I could take a month of my life and live at any time in the past, present, or future, I would choose to live it in the _____.

I say that because...

© 2005 Mindamics

12

32. Toolbox
Ten to Fourteen / Solo

No matter how rapidly technology changes our world, everyday life still requires frequent use of some old-fashioned, low-tech tools like the hammer, nail, screwdriver, screw, handsaw, level, tape measure, and sandpaper. Every daughter should be familiar with and comfortable using such tools, because she's going to have to repair stuff during her lifetime.

You can start off a very young child with a kid's toolbox, however I believe it's good to move on to the real McCoy as soon as she is able to handle it. Most girls can start hammering nails with some proficiency (after practice) around age six, and, with supervision, can handle a handsaw and drive screws with a screwdriver by around age eight or nine.

You and your daughter can help maintain enthusiasm for learning about good tool use by having a project under way. One traditional "first project" is a birdhouse, because it's reliably manageable (in other words, easy), quick, fun to do, and fun to use after you're finished. We'll steer you toward some birdhouse plans in a minute, but first some pointers on using hand tools.

The first rule with any tool is familiar and incontrovertible: Safety First! Always treat tools with respect, and hammer home this principle with your daughter. (No pun intended—well, actually, my daughters will insist that all my puns are intended.)

Safety First means using safety glasses or goggles while sawing or hammering, keeping your work area clean and uncluttered, securing things firmly while you're working on them, and providing lots of fatherly supervision.

Start teaching your daughter by using scrap wood that has been cleared of all nails, screws, staples, and other debris. White pine is a good beginner's wood, because it is fairly soft (and it's cheap). Pine two-by-fours are ideal for learning how to hammer, drive screws, measure, and saw.

How to Use a Hammer

The best starter hammer will have a striking surface that is flat. One old carpenter's trick is to run sandpaper crisscross over the surface every few days, which gives a better grip on the nails. Begin learning with flat-head nails. When your daughter is starting out, DON'T worry about making dents in the wood, or her ratio of misses to hits (as long as she is missing her thumb!), which is why you start on scrap wood.

At first you might want to hammer a small starter hole for her, since starting a nail is a tough thing to master. Then, have her hold the nail in place, center the hammer on the nail head, and begin tapping lightly. She'll readily see her progress, especially if the wood is soft.

After she has the swing of hitting the nail, slowly have her move her hand down the handle and lengthen the arc of her stroke, to generate more power. The eventual goal is to swing from the elbow and shoulder, keeping a firm wrist. Hold the hammer closer to its head for more precise work and farther down the handle for more swinging power.

Remember that practice is key. Give her a six foot long two-by-four of her very own, a box of flat-head nails, and let her go at it as long as she has the energy. Suggest that she make a pattern with her practice nails, like spelling out her initials or name.

How to Use a Handsaw

Good sawing requires that the saw operate as an extension of the arm. If the saw is too far out of proportion to the arm using it, the degree of difficulty rises. So begin with a short handsaw.

Since the saw is an extension of the arm, the sawyer should stand so that the shoulder, elbow, and hand are in line with the blade, and so that the hand pressure applied is in synch with the saw handle. To keep cuts straighter, keep your eye in the same plane as your saw, elbow, and shoulder.

Begin by setting the saw on the edge of the wood, and then draw the blade slowly toward you to start a cut where the blade can run smoothly—this cut is called a kerf. If you try to make a kerf by sawing away from your body, the saw will jump all over the place, make a mess, and you'll be very frustrated.

Once the kerf is formed (you can do this part for her at first), a few short, quick strokes will drive the blade deeper into the wood, and then you're on your way. Hand-sawing can seem (and sometimes actually be) a bit tedious, so emphasize patience with your daughter—and yourself—when it comes time to saw.

How to Use a Screwdriver

There really aren't many "instructions" one can provide for using a screwdriver. Remember "right-tighty, lefty-loosey," and that your daughter will need practice and patience (both hers and yours).

New technology has infiltrated the world of screwdrivers, with Phillips, Hex, Freason, Clutch head, Robertson square-tip, Bristol, and Torx heads now available—not to mention electric screwdrivers. You can find a good description of different screwdriver heads—with illustrations—at the Ace Hardware website—www.acehardware.com/sm-learn-about-screw drivers--bg-1266832.html.

Building a Birdhouse

Birdhouses are versatile because birds themselves are versatile. You can mount a birdhouse in the biggest city, the most rural neighborhood, and anywhere else birds fly—which is just about anywhere!

Since the dimensions of a birdhouse are fairly small, you and your daughter can build one using only hand tools. You might want to buy a simple birdhouse, take its measurements, and then try to duplicate it. Or you can turn to books or the Internet for guidance. A Castle Rock, Washington, company called L&R Designs offers an excellent (and free) birdhouse plan online at www.choosefreedom.com/freedownload/bh15 .pdf. The illustrations are clear and the instructions are easy to understand.

Here are some important guidelines for birdhouse building:

- Always use untreated lumber.
- Make sure the wood is thick enough to insulate the birds from cold and heat (at least three-quarter-inch thick) and will last a while.

- Leave the wood unpainted.
- Use galvanized screws to hold it together. Nails tend to rust and work loose, while glue breaks down in the weather.
- Consider making one wall (side or front) hinged, so you can clean out old nests each year.

Display your finished birdhouse prominently and proudly. Try to place it within sight of a house window or another location where you can observe birds using it year round.

When your daughter is comfortable and proficient using hand tools, you are convinced she respects them, and she's about twelve years old, move her up the tool ladder (another pun?) and begin teaching the proper use of power tools (see Power Tools Are a Girl's Best Friend on p. 149).

> **Tip:** When opening the world of tools to your daughter, open the world of wood, too. Go out in the neighborhood or nearby forest and examine different kinds of trees. Look at fallen trees to discover characteristics of the grain, color, and hardness. Then visit a lumber-yard to watch varieties of wood being cut, planed, stacked, and sold.

33. *She's the Coach: Friendship Bracelet*

Eleven to Fifteen / Solo and Group

Many girls already know how to make friendship bracelets, so this is a great chance for your daughter to teach you a thing or two. It's always a good learning experience when you teach someone else a skill. This activity has the added bonus of giving your daughter the pride of knowing that there's something she can do better than her hero.

To make the bracelets, you will need:

Clipboard
Embroidery thread
Scissors
Yardstick

- Choose two colors of embroidery thread. Cut three 27-inch strands of each color.
- Hold the ends of all six strands together and tie a knot about one inch from one end. Secure the knotted end by clipping it onto a clipboard. (Figure 1)
- Separate the colors so you have three strands of one color on the right and three strands of the other color on the left.
- Pick up the three strands on the left. Wrap them over and under all three strands on the right, forming a loop. (Figure 2)

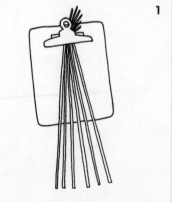

1

- Put the strands through the loop and pull tight, forming a single knot. (Figure 3) Pick up the three strands on the right. Wrap them over and under the strands on the left, forming a loop. Put the strands through the loop and pull tight, forming a knot. (Figure 4)
- Repeat the previous two steps until your bracelet is the desired length. (Figure 5)

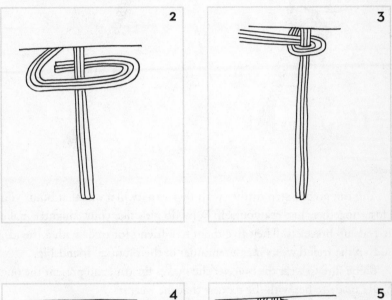

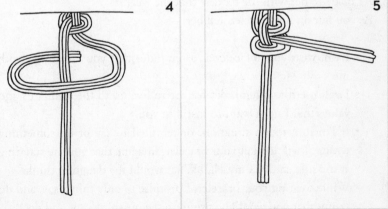

- Hold the ends of the strands together and tie a knot. (Figure 6)
- Trim the ends to about one inch. (Figure 7)

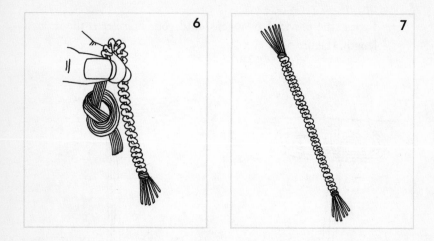

You can go one step further with this activity in a way that binds you closer together. Just ask yourself: Why do girls like your daughter make friendship bracelets? They give them to a friend (or trade with a friend), so that the friend wears it as a reminder of their mutual friendship.

So be sure to wear the bracelet she makes for you, and present the one YOU made to her with the request that she wear it.

As you put on her bracelet, tell her:

- I will wear your bracelet as a reminder that you are always with me.
- I will use it as a reminder for me to live up to the standards and values that I most want to instill in you.
- If I'm in a tough situation, or tempted to say or do something wrong, I will look at your bracelet, imagine that you are standing at my side, and ask myself, "What would my daughter think?"
- While wearing your bracelet, I promise to only think, say, and do things that you would be proud to see me think, say, and do.

Then, ask her if she is willing to make the same commitment while wearing the bracelet you made for her. The knot is a symbol of friendship, so when she wears the bracelet you've given her, you'll never be far from your daughter's thoughts. And in difficult situations, your bracelet on her wrist just might prompt her to consider, "What would my dad think?"

Group Activity

This is an extraordinary activity to do in a group of father-daughter pairs. The girls love the energy of showing their peers that they are more skilled at making the bracelets than Dad. Plus, it is quite moving to do the "presentation" ritual in a group.

Have all the daughters stand in a circle, facing outward, with their backs to each other. Position each dad so he is facing his daughter. You'll end up with a girls' circle inside the dads' circle.

The group leader then describes the significance of the bracelet, as explained in the "As you put on her bracelet, tell her" bullet points above.

Now, explain that each daughter will—one at a time—tie their bracelet onto their fathers' wrist while saying, "What I really admire about my father is _____." When every girl has spoken, then the dads will—one at a time—tie their bracelet onto their daughters' wrists while saying, "What I really admire about my daughter is _____."

> **Tip:** Making Friendship Bracelets is the most popular "tool" from my book *Dads & Daughters: How to Inspire, Understand, and Support Your Daughter,* and I graciously granted permission to reprint it! Check out the book as well as the Dads & Daughters website (www.dadsanddaughters.org) for more insight on having the best father-daughter relationship imaginable.

34. *Show Me the Money*
Ten to Eighteen / Solo

Joline Godfrey, author of *No More Frogs to Kiss: 99 Ways to Give Economic Power to Girls,* says that "financial literacy is not just about the money, but about launching great kids."

The world of work and money is a big part of our cultural heritage as men, so we're in an excellent position to share what we know with our daughters—who will have to manage money throughout their lives. For better or worse, we're the first ones they're likely to ask, so stepfathers and fathers have a real advantage in helping daughters be financially literate.

Here are two simple but very effective activities you and your daughter can do to learn about money—and each other:

Pay the Bills Together
Whether you pay your family bills every week or every month, include your daughter in the process. It is the single most concrete way to share your values about how and where you dedicate your resources.

Here are some simple tips to get her involved:

- Explain what the bills are for and how you pay them.
- Encourage her to ask any and all questions she has. One dad got stumped when his daughter asked how the water company could measure cubic feet when using round pipes. So they called the water company and both learned a lot about how that utility operates.
- Give her responsibility for some of the numbers—for example, adding and subtracting from your bank account or bill balances.
- Let her write out some or all of the checks before you sign them.
- Let her address and mail the envelopes, or learn to enter the data in your online bill-paying software.
- Teach her how to reconcile accounts, and then let her do it for you.

Her Own Checking Account

When our daughters were ten, we decided they were old enough to start learning simple lessons about managing money. Growing up (and even as young adults), neither Nancy nor I had a very good handle on that skill, so we figured if the girls started young, they'd be ahead of the game. We began with the basics. I took them to our local bank to open their own checking accounts. (I had no idea how strange some people would think this idea was—including the bank clerk.)

From then on, the girls handled their own income and expenses. Allowances, baby-sitting earnings, gift money, wages, quarters found on the sidewalk—it all went into the checking account. Nancy and I no longer paid for amusements or gifts for friends and family. We negotiated a clothing allowance by age twelve and put them in charge (sparking a sharp increase in shopping trips to Goodwill rather than to department stores). Even though they were young, the girls quickly adapted and we seldom heard them complain about it. They didn't spend much on themselves. They preferred, for example, to wait for birthdays to get clothes from grandparents and other relatives—a smart strategy, I always thought. Today, in their twenties, they are incredibly responsible.

Here are some simple ways to get and keep this going:

- Open a joint checking account with your daughter at your bank. There are few, if any, age restrictions, but most girls can handle the responsibility after age ten.
- Negotiate beforehand how you will handle any bounced checks. It's a rare person who has *never* bounced one, so settle on a deal like "I'll make you a bridge loan to cover the shortfall and penalty, but you have to pay me back within X amount of time."
- Negotiate an "allowance," and be clear that you consider it income for her.
- Negotiate with her what items and activities (e.g., clothes, entertainment, gifts for friends) she will be responsible for underwriting with that income, and then stick to the agreement. She may sometimes complain about not being able to afford something, but that's how money management works in real life. This dis-

comfort helps people learn how to cope, and she'll find that she can turn to things other than consumerism for enjoyment and satisfaction.

- Help her balance her checkbook the first few times, and then let her take the responsibility of doing it.
- Be available to discuss any of her money management questions or problems.
- Don't lecture; instead, help her see her options and think them through—even if she ends up choosing something that's not your first choice.
- Encourage her to choose a nonprofit to which she makes regular donations.

You both will be pleased with the sense of power, accomplishment, and responsibility that can grow out of this simple method of giving her accountability for her own money.

Resources

- The book *New Moon Money* (available at 800-381-4743) is edited by girls and filled with great tips, advice, and guidelines for managing money, creating budgets, starting a girl-run business, and much more.
- *No More Frogs to Kiss: 99 Ways to Give Economic Power to Girls* by Joline Godfrey (Collins, 1995) delivers on its title.
- Girls, Incorporated (the fabulous national nonprofit with the fabulous slogan "Strong, Smart, and Bold") has great tips and ideas for girls on its "Plan Ahead" webpage (www.girls-inc.org).
- Camp $tart-Up (www.independentmeans.com/imi/dollardiva/camp/index.php) helps teen women (ages 14–19) find ways to translate interests and dreams into enterprise and independence by meeting with each other and with successful women business owners.

35. Questing

Ten to Fifteen / Solo and Group

Questing is a wonderful way to communicate with your daughter in a fun, unusual way. Based on the British tradition of "letterboxing," questing is basically a sophisticated form of scavenger-hunting that can be done with just the two of you, or as part of a larger group.

Questing involves the use of containers called letterboxes that hold treats, messages, logbooks, and/or clues for finding the next letterbox in your hunt (or quest). Letterboxing began in the south of England in the 1850s, using canning jars to hold postcards, trinkets, and other small items.

One way to quest is by getting a group of other dads together to brainstorm simple "treasures" you can hide in letterboxes at locations around your neighborhood, around town, or out in wilder, natural surroundings.

For example, one dad organized a questing hiking expedition for a group of fathers and daughters. The dads put rubber stamps, nonfood treats, and pieces of paper with bits of fatherly wisdom in small Tupperware containers—their version of the letterbox. Then they hid the plastic containers along a hiking path in nearby mountains, after which they drew up clues to help their daughters find the hidden treasures.

You can present the clues through maps, rhyming riddles, written instructions, or even charade-like pantomimes. This activity works with girls of many ages—and if you're working with older girls, they can hide a series of letterboxes for the dads to find.

Questing participants let their creativity run wild. For example, some folks use the quest to guide participants to important cultural or historic locations around the community. Others dust off their old Boy Scout manuals and weave in elements of orienteering for the hunt.

One tradition in letterboxing is to leave your container in place, so that more than one person can find it over time. You can leave clues for anyone at the Letterboxing North America website. In this scenario, you leave a small "logbook" in your container, so that (once they find it) other people can write a note or mark the page with their personal rubber stamp. This tradition can make questing last for many years, as you and your daughter check back to see who has found your letterbox.

On a more individual quest, dads and daughters can make their own special items and messages to put in the letterboxes and create "how to find it" clues that are personal to their family. These letterbox messages are a great way to share important thoughts, feelings, and insights about each other and your relationship.

To celebrate the completion of your questing adventure, take your daughter—or the whole group of dads and daughters—out for breakfast or lunch at a favorite restaurant.

Or, plan a picnic as the culmination of your questing day. You could even make the picnic location the final destination given in the last clue.

At the Letterboxing North America website (www.letterboxing.org), you can find many resources including existing trails, ideas for carving a personalized stamp, cryptic clues, and details on "hitch-hikers"—letterboxes placed in another letterbox, and which are moved from box to box as they are found.

There are also tons of great ideas and examples in the book *Questing: A Guide to Creating Community Treasure Hunts* by Delia Clark and Steven Glazer (University Press of New England, 2004). You can hear a New Hampshire Public Radio interview with Clark and Glazer at www.nhpr .org/?q=node/7488/.

36. She's the Coach: Origami
Twelve to Sixteen / Solo and Group

A girl loves teaching her stepfather or father something that he doesn't already know. It makes her feel (justifiably) smart and proud. Here is one fairly common skill that girls are likely to know more about than their fathers and stepfathers. See this as a jumping-off point, however; be sure to tap into her interests and expertise together. My daughters are now in their twenties but still make paper cranes for fun, decorations, and to embellish gift wrapping.

The ancient Japanese art of origami seems to fascinate many preteen and teen girls. My daughters got hooked after reading a book about Sadako Sasaki, an athletic twelve-year-old Hiroshima girl who died of leukemia ten years after the first atom bomb was dropped. Sadako heard the old Japanese legend about the gods granting a wish to anyone who folds one thousand paper cranes. Hoping to get her wish for a cure, Sadako folded more than a thousand cranes in the months before she died.

Children all over the world still fold paper cranes in Sadako's honor and send them to Hiroshima Peace Park, where Japanese children paid to erect a statue of Sadako holding a golden crane, with the words THIS IS OUR CRY, THIS IS OUR PRAYER, PEACE IN THE WORLD inscribed on its base.

If your daughter already knows how to make some origami shapes, then ask her to teach you. You can make cranes, other animals, boxes, abstract shapes—the possibilities are endless. Plus, it's a wonderful, portable activity to do together while having a conversation, riding on a trip, listening to music, or watching TV.

If neither one of you know how to do origami, get a book or other resources so she can learn it herself. If she gets hooked and masters the skill, then she can teach you. The Origami-USA website has instructions for folding simple objects like cranes, butterflies, strawberries, and more at www.origami-usa.org/fold_this.html.

At our house, we liked books from the Klutz series. Their book *Origami* by Anne Akers Johnson includes excellent instructions and lots of paper. (You might also check out the Klutz book *Twisted Paper* by Jacqueline Lee, which shows how to make hundreds of objects from simple strips of paper—not origami, but lots of fun!)

Tip: If you and your daughter want some of your paper cranes to hang near Sadako's memorial, string them on a garland of string (with a loop at the end for hanging) and mail them to General Affairs Division, Hiroshima Peace Culture Foundation, 1–2 Nakajima-cho, Naka-ku, Hiroshima, Japan 730-0811. For more info, visit the official homepage of the Hiroshima Peace Memorial Museum at www.pcf.city.hiroshima.jp/index_e2.html.

37. Ten Famous Women
Ten to Fifteen / Solo and Group

Of all the activities and workshops I do around the country for fathers and daughters, Ten Famous Women is the most difficult for daughters and dads to complete.

I ask the father-daughter pairs to name ten famous women—but without including any contemporary singers, actors, or performers. Eliminating celebrities makes it a hard list for most people to compile, and it reveals two important truths:

1. Girls and women are still very likely to achieve fame for their looks or for relatively fleeting accomplishments (like being a pop star).
2. Girls and women are still fairly invisible in the halls of history and the halls of decision-making.

This activity is simple: Leaving off any current celebrities, list ten famous women, and a brief description of why they are famous.

You can do this as a friendly competition between daughter and father or in a group of daughter-father pairs. You can base the competition on any one of these factors:

Who finishes their list first.
Who has women from the widest range of historical eras.
Who has the most unique names—names that no one else has on their list.
Who has the most names of women from outside your home country.

To provide an example, I've listed ten women who made substantial contributions to history.

Mary Tsukamoto: a teacher who worked to get the U.S. government to compensate Japanese-American families (like her own) who were interned in prison camps during World War II.

Patsy Mink: the first woman of color to serve in the U.S. Congress. A longtime Hawaiian congresswoman, she was a primary sponsor of Title IX, the civil rights statute outlawing gender discrimination in American education.

Debi Thomas: the first African-American woman to win a gold medal in a world figure-skating competition.

Juana Gutierrez: influential Los Angeles community organizer who helped create the Madres de Este Los Angeles (MELASI).

Janet Guthrie: pilot, flight instructor, and aerospace engineer who became the first woman to drive a race car in the Indianapolis 500 and Daytona 500 (both in 1977).

Mary Taylor Previte: spent seven years in a World War II Japanese POW camp, and then used the experience to create a national juvenile justice model for helping teenagers at the Camden County (New Jersey) Youth Center.

Jeannette Rankin: first woman elected to the U.S. Congress (Republican from Montana), years before women were granted the right to vote nationally.

Geraldyn (Jerrie) Cobb: first woman to pass qualifying exams for astronaut training, in 1959. But this famous pilot was kept out of the space program because she was a woman.

Dorothy Height: president of the National Council of Negro Women for more than forty years.

Maria Tallchief: daughter of an Osage chief, she was prima ballerina of the New York City Ballet and founded the Chicago City Ballet with her sister, Marjorie.

How many of these women had you heard of? Your answer may tell you how hard it is to find famous women on the ordinary person's radar.

The first time you do Ten Famous Women, you and your daughter can each borrow one of the women on my list. Then, head off into the exciting and fascinating world of women who made a difference.

Here are some excellent online resources for uncovering women's history heroes:

- National Women's History Project, www.nwhp.org. NWHP also has a fabulous links page that can connect you with dozens and dozens of other sites on almost every aspect of women's history: www.nwhp.org/tlp/links/links.html
- The (U.S.) National Archives—www.archives.gov/research/alic/reference/women.html
- Library and Archives Canada—www.collectionscanada.ca/women/index-e.html
- National Women's History Museum—www.nmwh.org (also working toward a wonderful bricks-and-mortar museum in Washington, D.C.—go visit!)

38. Way Back Days

Nine to Fifteen / Solo and Group

In one of my favorite movies, writer/director John Hughes gives Ferris Bueller the following line: "Life moves pretty fast. If you don't stop and look around once in a while, you could miss it." That's a very important thing to remember when raising a daughter.

One fun way to stop and look around at life is to step back toward a time when life didn't move at the supersonic speed of today. Fortunately, it's easy to do this by tapping into girls' interest in historical eras. For example, my daughters spent years fascinated by Jane Austen novels, living history museums, and American Girl dolls, which portray different periods in U.S. history.

In the Way Back Day activity, you don't need a time machine. Instead, pick a period in history that your daughter or stepdaughter finds interesting, and then spend a day (or part of a day) recreating what daily life might have been like for your family during that era.

One of my daughters had the American Girl doll named Molly. Molly's back-story was that she grew up in the U.S. during World War II. Here are some things you could do to play life for a family on the home front during the 1940s.

Roller-skate with traditional strap-on skates.

Play checkers.

Get old-time radio shows on tape or CD from the library, or from the Internet, and play them during the evening instead of watching TV.

Pretend you've used up your entire book of gasoline ration stamps, and walk or ride bikes everywhere during that day.

Have a "rationed" dinner made up of canned food.

"Black out" some of your windows with black construction paper.

Dress up in clothes from the 1940s (you've always wanted to wear a fedora, haven't you?)—thrift shops are good places to search.

Read children's books or comics from the period.

Watch a famous movie from or about the forties, like *His Girl Friday* or *The Philadelphia Story*.

My daughter Nia was so fascinated with history, women's historical roles, and the evolution of clothing that she got her college degree in costume design and literature. Nia was (and still is) a huge Jane Austen fan. Here are some travel-back-in-time activities we could have done on a "pretend we've living in early nineteenth-century England" day, had we thought of this activity fifteen years ago:

Eat only foods that we've prepared from scratch.

Play whist (rules at www.pagat.com/whist/whist.html).

Find costumes or fancy-up existing clothing to make it look like fashion from the Regency period (see dresses at www.pemberley.com/janeinfo/ppbrokil.html#gencloth).

Speak like an Austen character or Austen herself. Here are some deliciously profound and/or ironic lines from her letters:

I do not think it worth while to wait for enjoyment until there is some real opportunity for it.

Next week [I] shall begin my operations on my hat, on which you know my principal hopes of happiness depend.

I do not want people to be very agreeable, as it saves me the trouble of liking them a great deal.

I could not sit seriously down to write a serious romance under any other motive than to save my life; and if it were indispensable for me to keep it up and never relax into laughing at myself or other people, I am sure I should be hung before I had finished the first chapter.

This exquisite weather is too good . . . I enjoy it all over me, from top to toe, from right to left, longitudinally, perpendicularly, diago-

nally; and I cannot but selfishly hope we are to have it last till Christmas—nice, unwholesome, unseasonable, relaxing, close, muggy weather.

Write clever letters to each other and to other relatives.
Play music by Handel, Mozart, and Beethoven.
Go for a long walk while conversing with each other.
Read to each other out loud from *Pride and Prejudice*.

These are just starter ideas. Pick any period in history and do a little research about the foods, daily habits, language, and entertainments of the time. Then recreate as much of it as you want during your Way Back Day.

Share stories and photos of your own activity on the *Dads & Daughters Togetherness Guide* website (see p. 168).

> **Tip:** Have a Way Back Day that re-creates what it was like when you were your daughter's age. What meals did you eat? What did you do for entertainment? How did you spend your time after school or on a summer day? You'll be surprised at how different—or even exotic—that life may seem to your daughter. "You mean you actually lived without iPods and websites? You only had three TV channels? And you had to get up and go over to the TV to change the channels?"

39. She's the Coach: Knit and Crochet

Twelve to Eighteen / Solo and Group

Yes, a girl can teach her old stepfather or father a new trick or two. There really are some skills she is likely to be more expert in than Dad. She feels smart and proud when she has the chance to show off that expertise. For example, girls may know more about knitting and crocheting than their fathers and stepfathers. See this as a jumping-off point, however; be sure to tap into her interests and expertise together.

My daughter Mavis and my sister Ellen are avid knitters. My wife, Nancy, and daughter Nia dabble in knitting and crocheting. All of them have attempted to teach me how to learn this simple skill, but I never caught on. I think that's because I lack patience. As I always tell them, "If I wanted to learn patience, I would have made time for it!"

Well, don't let me be your example here. Knitting is an incredibly low-tech, portable, satisfying, fun, and gender-blind activity. Crocheting is even more low-tech (it requires only one needle to knitting's two).

Tween and teen girls are likely to have picked up knitting from friends or (usually female) relatives. But again, if she doesn't know how to knit or crochet, hook her up (get the pun?) with some books and websites. The Klutz book *Knitting*, also by Anne Akers Johnson, takes her from step zero (how to hold the needles and yarn) to finished projects she'll show off shamelessly. You and she can also turn to *Knitting for Dummies* and *Crocheting for Dummies*, or *The Complete Idiot's Guide to Knitting & Crocheting* by Gail Diven.

The Craft Yarn Council of America has a comprehensive website to teach anyone how to knit or crochet at www.learntoknit.com/home .html. It includes basic instructions (with illustrations) of how to do basic knitting and crocheting stitches as well as simple projects to encourage more practice.

If you own a cat, yarn crafts hold the extra bonus of watching the cat play with the balls of yarn—and trying to keep the yarn away from the cat while you're knitting!

40. *Industrial Inquiry*
Eight to Thirteen / Solo and Group

Although I'm not terribly skilled in using them, I love tools. I also love looking at small machines, medium-sized machines, really big machines, and factories. A lot of guys grow up fascinated by how things work, how things are made, and what goes on behind the scenes of a business or manufacturer.

Our daughters can be fascinated by this sort of thing as well. My daughters loved seeing the backstage of our local community theater and ballet performances. In junior high they started volunteering to build sets and props and make costumes.

Big and Brawny

Even if they don't develop a lifelong interest, it's still fun to visit factories nearby or as part of a vacation trip. You can make a tour extra special if it's a day set aside for just the two of you, and you add special touches like going out to eat. Your best bet is to come up with a list of possible places to visit and let her make the final choice.

There are more factory tours available than you might think. Here are just a fraction of those open to visitors in one state, Pennsylvania:

Crayola Crayons, Easton
Harley-Davidson, York
Hershey Chocolate, Hershey
Ingersoll-Rand construction equipment, Shippensburg
Martin Guitar, Nazareth
Susquehanna Glass Company, Columbia
U.S. Mint, Philadelphia
Zippo lighters and Case cutlery, Bradford

And here's a taste of industry tours in Hawaii:

Mauna Loa (Macadamia Nuts), Hilo
Big Wind Kite Factory, Mauna Loa
Big Island Candies, Hilo
Ueshima Coffee Company, Captain Cook
Maui Divers, Honolulu
Dole Pineapple Plantation, rural Oahu

Many sports stadiums and arenas have behind-the-scenes tours, where you can learn how stadium crews switch the playing surface from ice hockey to basketball, or from football to baseball—all in a matter of a few hours.

You can learn about hundreds of factory tours (from Boeing in Washington to the Spam Museum in Minnesota) at http://factorytoursusa.com or in books like *Watch It Made in the U.S.A.* by Karen Axelrod and Bruce Brumberg (Avalon Travel Publishing, 2002).

Close to Home

If you don't live near a big factory (or if you've seen all of them in your area), don't overlook smaller local businesses, which can be just as fascinating. When New York father Bob Stien's daughters were smaller, he took them to see business operations close to home, including a beekeeper, a bowling alley, an apple cider bottler, and a tofu maker.

They hit it off so well with the apple cider bottler that they went back each fall to help him process the fall harvest! Bob says he was amazed at how receptive people are to showing us what they do and how they do it. Whenever he read an article in his local newspaper about an interesting business, he'd call them up and ask if he and his girls could explore their operation. Business owners and craftspeople said they seldom got those kinds of calls, and they were almost universally thrilled by the interest. After all, who doesn't like getting to play the expert and showing off their accomplishments?

Other close-to-home places to explore include:

Fire station

Police station

Bookstore

Newspaper

TV and/or radio stations

Florist

Bakery

Pet store

Community artist studios (painters, photographers, weavers, potters, etc.)

Utilities (electric company, wastewater plant, waste disposal plant, water company)

Take Her to Work

One obvious nearby workplace is your own. I encourage every dad to participate in Take Our Daughters and Sons to Work Day (www.daughtersandsonstowork.org) on the fourth Tuesday of April. But you can bring her to work other days, too. You might be surprised by the impact.

When I was a preteen, my father worked at a now-defunct Philadelphia department store called Lit Brothers. Dad was a buyer and had an office in among the stock shelves just off the sales floor. Once or twice a year, my older sisters and I would each get a day alone at work with him. He'd take me to lunch at Lit Brothers' dining room. At age nine, linen napkins with my grilled cheese sandwich seemed like the height of elegance. I'd see the bright lights of the sales floor and the finely dressed saleswomen, then wander around the dim warren of shelving and desks in the windowless stockroom, feeling as though I were backstage at an elaborate theatrical production.

I'm sure my father never thought his job resembled Broadway, but it did in my childhood eyes. Those memories are vivid because, when he took me to work with him, my father gave me a glimpse into what he did all day and where he spent so much of his energy and creativity—something I couldn't see otherwise.

I tried to carry that tradition on as a father. My daughters still remember their visits to the radio station where I worked when they were young. They loved seeing all the gear and gizmos that made it possible for them to hear their father's voice come out of the little plastic kitchen radio while they ate their breakfast.

You don't need to work someplace exotic or cool for your workplace to be exciting to your daughter. One of my editors at Broadway Books loved visiting her dad's office as a girl. His was a pretty basic office, but she still loved playing with paper clips and the copier, riding the subway, meeting his colleagues, having lunch with him, calling Mom from "the office," and carrying Dad's briefcase home for him. No matter what your job, it is nice, satisfying, and exciting for your daughter to see what your work world is about.

Research shows that successful adult women frequently credit their drive and ambition to their fathers. Among the important things dads did for these daughters was take them to their own work (regardless of what kind of work it was), talk about their own work, hold the daughters to high standards, and encourage them to take risks.

But no matter what form it takes, the best part of Industrial Inquiry is how much fun it is for dad and daughter!

41. *Go Mobile*
Nine to Fourteen / Solo and Group

Must you live in Alabama to be excited about Mobiles? Of course not!

The beautiful and influential art form of mobiles was invented by U.S. engineer and sculptor Alexander Calder in the 1930s. One of its greatest beauties is the relative ease with which anyone can create a simple mobile.

This father-daughter activity combines creativity with the scientific method (otherwise known, in my own father's words, as "trial and error"). As Anne and Christopher Moorey write in their 1966 book *Making Mobiles*, "Although it is fairly easy to produce a mobile that is technically balanced, it is much harder to balance the forms in a way that is satisfying to look at."

One can try endless variations of mobiles, or nearly endless variations of the same mobile. Combine that with the ability to make them with inexpensive materials (like coat hangers, construction paper, and straws), and you've got an ideal father-daughter activity!

Simple for Starters
Materials:
Drinking straws
Paper clips
Tape
Construction paper and scissors

Use this method with younger girls, because it's easier for them to manipulate the materials, and there is less chance of her (or you) getting poked.

Decide on shapes you want to hang from the mobile (animals, stars, circles onto which you glue photos of family members, etc.), and cut between four and ten of those shapes out of construction paper—making sure each shape is roughly the same size and weight. (Figure 1)

Take a standard drinking straw and slip three paper clips onto it—one in the middle, and one about a half inch in from either end. The middle paper clip is your pivot for the entire mobile. We'll identify this as straw #1. (Figure 2)

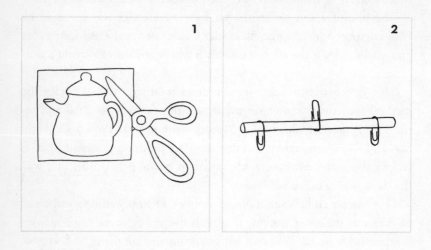

To make the simplest, most symmetrical mobile, add two more paper clips to each of the clips hanging from the ends of straw # 1. Then create two more straws exactly like straw #1. We'll call these straw #2 and straw #3. Attach the middle clip on straw #2 to the string of three paper clips on the left side of straw #1, and attach the middle clip on straw #3 to the string of three paper clips on the right side of straw #1. (Figure 3)

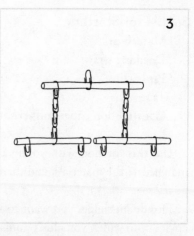

Now add two or three more paper clips to the clips on either end of straw #2 and straw #3. At the end of these four strings of paper clips, attach four of the construction paper shapes you cut out. It helps to also tape the figures to the paper clip, to make sure they don't slip off. (Figure 4)

Finally, tie a string through the middle (pivot) paper clip on straw #1 and hang your mobile up. You will probably have to adjust where the paper clip strings are located on each straw to achieve balance. Once it looks right, stabilize everything by taping the paper clip strings in place on their respective straws. (Figure 5)

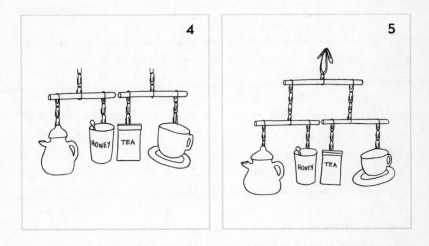

To make a more complicated version, use the same techniques, but break up the symmetry. For example, put a six-paper-clip string between straw #1 and straw #2. On straw #3, instead of attaching the two cutout figures, attach two more straws (#4 and #5), each with the same paper clip arrangement as the other straws.

Add two more paper clips on each end of both straw #4 and straw #5, and then attach cutout figures to those paper clip strings—giving you a total of six cutout figures. Again, you'll have to play around with the weights and balances to get your desired results—but that's half the fun!

More Complex and Daring
Materials:
Wire clothes hangers

Picture wire (or sturdy string)

Material for shapes (construction paper, cardboard, wood, or sheet metal)

Wire cutters

Pliers

Tool for cutting out shapes (scissors, tin snips, etc.)

This method relies on the same principles of physics as the straw-and-paper-clip method, but uses sturdier materials and more planes (of the geometric variety), which gives you greater design flexibility.

Using wire cutters, cut one-foot lengths from the bottom of six wire coat hangers. Dad should handle this chore, unless daughter has mastered the skills in Toolbox (p. 100). At both ends of each piece of hanger wire, use pliers (needle-nose are best) to make a small loop, making sure that no sharp edges are exposed.

Use the pliers to make a small loop in the center of hanger wire #1. Then thread hanger wire #2 through that loop and bend it around into a loop that intertwines with the center loop of hanger wire #1. Notice that in this structure, your top "layer" is two pieces forming an X, unlike the straw method, where the top layer is only one piece creating only one plane.

Create four more hanger wires (#3 through #6) with the same design as hanger wire #1—small loops at either end and a small loop in the center.

Next, use a length of picture wire (or sturdy string) to attach the center loop on hanger wire #3 to the end loop on the left end of hanger wire #1. Use picture wire of the same length to attach the center loop on hanger wire #4 to the end loop on the right end of hanger wire #1. Use picture wire of the same length to attach the center loop on hanger wire #5 to the loop on the left end of hanger wire #2. Use picture wire of the same length to attach the center loop on hanger wire #6 to the loop on the right end of hanger wire #2.

Now, hang equal lengths of picture wire (or sturdy string) down from the loops on the ends of hanger wires #3 through #6. Use that picture wire to attach your shapes to the mobile, and then adjust for weight and balance.

The center loop in hanger wire #1, in addition to holding hanger wire #2 in place, also serves as the mobile's central pivot point, so that's where you tie the picture wire that connects the entire structure to the ceiling.

For a less complicated variation, you can skip the second layer of hanger wires and simply attach four cutout shapes directly to wires tied to the end loops on hanger wires #1 and #2. For a more complex version, vary the lengths of the picture wire (like you did with the second version of the straw-and-paper-clip method) and/or add additional layers of hanger wires and cutouts.

Since the supporting hanger wire is heavier, you have the freedom to use heavier materials to make your shapes of stars, animals, abstract forms, or other ideas. You can use construction paper, but the mobile is likely to have more visual balance if you use more substantial material, like cardboard, plywood, or cutout pieces of sheet metal. IMPORTANT: When working with and cutting sheet metal (no matter what your age), always wear gloves and safety goggles.

On the Enchanted Learning website (www.enchantedlearning.com/crafts/mobiles/), you can see diagrams of simple mobiles to make at home.

If you want to go math-wild, you can download a diagram to create a 3-D mobile using algebraic equations at www.teachervision.fen.com/algebra/printable/7284.html.

You can see photos of Calder's own mobiles at www.calder.org and learn how to make a mobile inspired by his design at www.sdmart.org/pix/education/Calder.pdf.

Tip: As you get more daring and complex in your designs, mobile artist Tim Rose says the secret is to start at the bottom and work toward the top. Lay out your shapes on a large piece of paper, with the smallest ones along a straight line on the bottom. Then draw lines to the figures on the next row or layer, and repeat as you go up. This gives you guidance on how to do your wiring or stringing and allows you to address some balance issues before you get into the nitty-gritty of construction.

One thing I'm really proud of is _____.

I say that because...

© 2004 Mindamics

42. The Mount Pisgah Hike
Nine to Fourteen / Group

You mean you don't know where Mount Pisgah is? There are Mount Pisgahs in Oregon, New York, Pennsylvania, and North Carolina's Blue Ridge mountains—all named for the biblical mountain where Moses saw the Promised Land before he died.

There is good news, though: You don't need a Mount Pisgah to do this activity. In fact, you can do it anywhere that offers a simple, not-too-challenging, three-to-four-hour hike in nature. Use a hill, forest, field, national park, or even a large city park.

I named this activity The Mount Pisgah Hike because it describes how Asheville, North Carolina, father Scott MacGregor organized a group of second-grade girls and their fathers to walk up the Blue Ridge Mount Pisgah.

This group activity can be organized by one father or by a group of dads. It is best done on a weekend or holiday, running from about ten in the morning to two or three in the afternoon, including all travel to and from the hike location.

When making the arrangements beforehand, the organizer(s) should hike the trail ahead of time (at least a week before) to pick out the best spots for each stop on the trek. If at all possible, get a map of the area where you'll be hiking. If you have copies of a map, you can add a small element of orienteering to your hike.

Pre-Hike Prep

Have the following supplies on hand for the day of the hike:

Snacks for each hiker, including protein sources (nuts, cheese sticks) and energy sources (candy bars). Skip anything salty! *Note:* You will need enough for two snack breaks and a lunch break, but keep it simple.

A two-to-three-foot length of rope for each hiker.

One carabiner for each father-daughter pair.

A digital camera.

Instruct each hiker to bring:

Comfortable hiking shoes.

Comfortable clothes (including gear to handle any inclement weather).

A small backpack.

A journal (or pad of paper) and a working pen.

A working whistle (or other agreed-upon device for making a loud noise).

Nalgene bottles or canteens of water—at least a half gallon each.

A compass (if you decide to use the maps).

Meeting Up

At ten o'clock Saturday morning, everyone meets in the school parking lot (or another central location). Then you carpool and caravan to the hike location. Once you get there, gather everyone together to hear the ground rules:

1. Safety First
   A. Be alert—don't get hurt. Go slow and steady.
   B. Your whistle is for safety. It is not a toy—use it only if you are lost or in trouble.
   C. Let's give the whistles a loud, rowdy blow right now. That tests them—and releases our urge to blow them for fun.
   D. If you get lost: Breathe, stay put, listen, and whistle.

2. Have fun; enjoy the hike/journey.

3. Show respect for others and nature.
   A. Golden rules: Everybody's included, and do unto others as you would have them do unto you.

B. Stay on the trail.

C. If you have to go to the bathroom, get Dad and go.

4. Teamwork.

A. Be a good leader; slow and steady with Dad.

Now, let's start hiking!

> **Tip:** Scott suggests: "For the hiking itself, I had two bandanas: one red and one green. Each girl got to be the group leader at the front (green bandana) and pull up the rear (red bandana). No one (including dads) could go ahead or behind these bandanas. This gave the girls a nice sense of empowerment."

Stop #1: Map & Compass

Describe how to use the compass and map to orient yourself, specifically so you can find the start and finish of the hike should you get lost or separated from the group. Note: You should do everything you can to keep the group together throughout the hike, so there is little likelihood anyone will have to use their orienteering skills. But this step of preparation adds to the sense of adventure for everyone.

Stop #2: You and Dad

Have everyone sit down comfortably and pull out their pens and paper. Explain that you will be asking a series of questions, and that the responsibilities are as follows:

> Daughters should write their answers to the questions in their journal.
>
> Dad is free to jot down his thoughts and reactions to the questions, too—but he keeps completely quiet while his daughter is working.
>
> When the daughters are done writing their answers, they will talk about them one-on-one with their dads.

The dads' *most* important job is to listen to what the daughters say. Don't defend or explain yourself—rather, listen very closely so that you can hear and understand everything your daughter is telling you.

Here are the questions:

What is the first thing you remember about your dad?
I really love it when my dad does _____ with me.
My dad shows me he cares when he does _____ for me.
Boy, it really makes me mad when my dad does _____.

Once the girls are done sharing their answers and insights with the fathers, pack up for the next stage of the hike.

Stop #3: Observe-o-rama

Have everyone sit down comfortably and pull out their pens and paper. Instruct everyone to be perfectly still and quiet for three minutes—except for writing down their answers to these questions:

What can you see around you?
What can you hear around you?
What can you smell?
From where you are sitting, what can you feel with your sense of touch?
How do you feel inside?

When the three minutes are up, have the fathers and daughters share their observations with each other—reminding the dads that their *most* important job is to listen.

When done, break out some of the snacks!

Stop #4: Specialties

Have everyone sit down comfortably and pull out their pens and paper. Ask them all to finish the statement: "I am special because _____," and take two minutes so they can write down their responses.

Ask the daughters to finish the statement, "My dad is special to me because _____," and take two minutes to have them write down their responses.

Simultaneously, ask the dads to finish the statement, "My daughter is special to me because _____," and take two minutes so they can write down their responses.

When everyone is finished, have the fathers and daughters share their observations with each other—reminding the dads that their *most* important job is to listen.

The Top of the Mountain! (or, the Midway Point)

Celebrate reaching the top of the mountain, or the midway point of your hike. Lead everyone in a "We did it!" shout or cheer. Then, sit down and have lunch.

When lunch is finished and everything is cleaned up, gather everyone together for a group photograph. Take a bunch of shots, so you'll have some to choose from—because you'll be sending everyone a copy of the best one later on.

Last, talk about getting back down the mountain or the trail. Explain that it is still *very* important to go slow and steady and to work together, because we're going to be more tired than when we started out.

Now, go back down the mountain or head off on the last half of the trail.

Stop #5: Ropes & Carabiners

Instruct each daughter to "Come get one of the carabiners, and a rope for you and one for your dad."

Have everyone sit down comfortably and pull out their pens and paper.

Write/talk about a time when your dad made you feel safe.

Write/talk about a time when you made Dad feel safe/cared for.

Again, the fathers' main job is to listen and hear what the daughters have to say. When that discussion is finished, explain that each daughter and each dad are different people with unique characteristics and strengths. Say "Your piece of rope represents the special person you are. The carabiner represents the special father-daughter bond you have."

Instruct each daughter and father to tie their rope onto opposite sides of their carabiner. Then describe how a carabiner—even though it looks small—can hold hundreds and hundreds of pounds of weight. Just like your daughter-father relationship, the carabiner is portable, tough, reliable, lasts a long time, and is flexible enough to be used in many different locations and circumstances.

Finally, explain that each person chose to tie their rope to the carabiner, just like you choose to bond together as daughter and father. You need to care for the rope, the knots, and the carabiner so that they will stay strong. Encourage the father-daughter pairs to keep the rope-carabiner combination in a visible place back at home, where they can see it and be reminded of how important and special their own daughter-father bond is.

Stop #6: The Magic Wand

Have everyone sit down comfortably and pull out their pens and paper. Have each girl write down "three things you would want to do with your dad if you had a magic wand." Then the daughters share their answers with their dads—and the fathers remember that their most important job is to listen.

Stop #7: The End of the Trail

When you reach the trailhead—and before getting back into the cars and driving away—wrap the event up with one more simple activity. Have everyone sit down comfortably. Then invite each daughter to introduce her dad to the group and tell everyone one neat thing about him. Then have each dad introduce his daughter to the group and tell everyone one neat thing about her.

Next, have the girls gather in a group and chant together, "I love it when my dad listens to me!" Then, have the dads gather in a group and chant together, "I love listening to my daughter!"

Thank everyone for being there and climb back into the cars for the drive back home.

> **Tip:** This activity takes good planning ahead and a fair amount of logistical coordination. But it will be such a hit, you will have fathers clamoring for an encore next year.

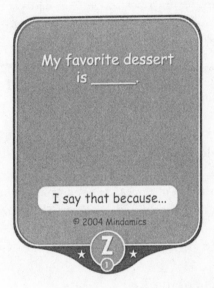

Teens

Modern teenagers can have incredibly busy lives: heavy school loads, friends, sports, volunteering, music, extracurricular activities, romances, and more. It seems like weeks often pass without time for a conversation that isn't exclusively about chores, crises, or logistics.

It may look to you like your daughter or stepdaughter doesn't have much space in her life for you anymore. But looks can be deceiving. When my daughters moved into their teen years, my vision was often clouded by fears for their safety and fear that a fateful reckoning day—when they grew up and moved away—was fast approaching on the horizon.

A bit of fear can be a healthy motivator, but can also dominate our view of things before we know it. Fortunately, play and fear tend to be mutually exclusive (with the exception of riding a roller coaster). So a regular diet of fun can drive out fear and nourish the open, authentic connection that we crave with our daughters—and that they (sometimes secretly) crave with us.

Remember: Just because she's growing up fast doesn't mean either one of you has to abdicate "Our Time" (p. 12) together.

Plus, now that your daughter is approaching adulthood, there are many more adult activities and interests to share. So take advantage of the new ways to connect with and enjoy each other. No matter how old she gets, she'll still have times when she needs her dad and stepdad. That's why it's so important for her stepdad and/or dad to be fully present in her life—even during adolescence.

(continued)

The teens section contains activities to help build the father-daughter connection on a more sophisticated level, one that respects and responds to the person she is becoming.

So keep making time to have fun and make memories together!

43. *Heritage Interview*
Fourteen to Eighteen / Solo

Each of us holds a place in the history of our own families. But we also hold a place in the history of the world in which we live. It's fun to explore the ways in which those places intersect. When exploring it with your daughter, you both learn a bit more about how you got to be who you are today.

When I was nine years old, three civil rights workers—James Chaney, Andrew Goodman, and Michael Schwerner—were murdered in Philadelphia, Mississippi. I still remember watching the news and talking about the murders around the family dinner table as the story of violence, racism, and local police cover-up unfolded.

Almost forty years later, my daughter Mavis took a course on civil rights from Michael Schwerner's brother, Steve, a professor at Antioch College in Ohio. At the beginning of the course, Dr. Schwerner instructed his students to write a paper on how each of them came to hold their moral value system. He told them to begin by interviewing parents and grandparents to uncover their own families' values heritage.

When Mavis called to interview me, it was one of the most fascinating conversations we ever had. I ended up telling her stories about my parents, grandparents, and other relatives—stories that she'd never heard before. Plus, it forced me to think about the individuals, values, and beliefs I observed in my ancestors—and which ones inspired me the most growing up and still today.

Use the following questions as kickoffs to an interview or conversation with each other about what you see as the roots of your deepest values and beliefs. Some of these questions will work for both of you, and others will be more suited for your stepdaughter or daughter to ask you.

Describe an experience that demonstrates your character.
Describe an experience that helped shape your character.
What are the three most important values to you in a relationship?

What did your father and other male relatives or ancestors teach you about relationships?

What did your mother and other female relatives teach you?

Describe the two most satisfying experiences of your life.

Describe the two times in your life when you feel you made your biggest contribution to the community.

What are the three values you hold most dear as a member of your community? As a citizen of the world?

Name three relatives or ancestors who influenced your belief system the most.

How and why do you think their example influenced you so much?

How would you describe your values and moral heritage?

Tip: Keep your answers and insights in your DDPJ (see p. 24).

44. She's the Coach: Podcasting
Fourteen to Sixteen / Solo

One of a girl's greatest thrills is to teach her stepfather or father something that he doesn't already know. It makes her feel (justifiably) smart and proud. Fortunately, today's world provides us with a variety of technology, crafts, sports, activities, music, and more that girls know more about than we do. So find areas of interest where she is more expert than you, and tell her that you want her to lead your exploration of them.

Podcasting is one fairly common skill that girls are likely to know more about than their fathers and stepfathers. See this as just a jumping-off point, however; be sure to tap into a variety of her interests and expertise together.

A podcast is basically a broadcast that you can send out over the World Wide Web. That may sound intimidating—and it is a little, but less than you might think. First off, your "broadcast" can be any length—even one minute. Second, the software and equipment needed to do it are fairly inexpensive, and if you have a computer, it may be already loaded with everything you need. Third, podcasts can be anything from simple audio to sophisticated video. Fourth, if your daughter knows much about computers, Mp3 files, iPods, and the rest—then she probably knows most of what you both need to become adequate (if not brilliant) podcasters.

So get out the microphone and/or webcam and start creating something together. You can record the latest family news and then share those podcasts with relatives and friends around the country. You can record or act out the creations you wrote in Papa Poetry (p. 74). You can sing or play music. And, you can even find blogging services on the web to host your podcasts for free or for very little money. A good place to

start learning the technical ins and outs is at this website: www.ftp
planet.com/blog_guide/podcasting.htm.

By the way, if this information becomes obsolete in the months between my writing and your reading, chalk it up to the world passing us
old fogies by!

45. The Art of Giving and Asking
Fourteen to Eighteen / Solo

Most of our parents worked to instill in us the value of giving to others, and we're probably trying to instill the same values in our children and stepchildren. This activity provides a way for both of you to explore more deeply what it means to give help, and what it means to ask for help. It was inspired by Rich Snowden of California, a life coach and Dads & Daughters volunteer.

Many of us guys (me included) have a hard time asking for help. Many girls in our culture also have a hard time asking for help—at least without feeling obligated to sacrifice essential parts of their identity in the process. So the two sides of giving and asking for help are important areas to think and talk about together.

On separate pieces of paper, you and your daughter answer the following questions for yourselves. When you're done, swap papers and discuss your answers. Work to make this a learning experience instead of a teaching one—in other words, strive to learn more about how you and she each conceptualize giving and asking for help rather than instructing her (at least for now) on what you think her attitudes *should* be.

What are three of your favorite experiences with giving?

Thinking about the time when you gave most generously or extravagantly to someone else, what inspired you? Describe how that felt.

How do you like to be asked for help? Are there times when you feel sincerely happy about being asked?

How much do you like to be asked by someone versus deciding to give on your own initiative?

How do you like to be thanked for what you give?

Do you use giving to express yourself? How is giving a way of openly expressing what matters to you and what you believe in?

What are three of your least favorite experiences with giving?

Have you ever wanted to ask to get your gift or generosity back? Have you ever actually done it?

How often do you say yes to giving help, when you really want to say no? Why do you say yes when you want to say no? When was a time that the person asking made it easy to say no and you said no?

Remember a time when you've had to ask for help and it was hard to do so. What was hard about it?

Remember a time when you've had to ask for help, and it was easy to do so. What was easy about it?

As a child, when did you first become aware of the idea and benefits of giving to others? What did you see? What were you curious about?

As a child, when did you first become aware of the idea and benefits of asking others for help? What did you see? What were you curious about?

Do you give mostly with your head or your heart? Or both?

Tip: You don't have to answer all of these questions in one sitting. Feel free to break them up into smaller chunks and do them over time. Save your answers in your DDPJ (see p. 24).

46. Power Tools Are a Girl's Best Friend

Fourteen to Eighteen / Solo and Group

This activity takes its name from a delightful song by singer-songwriter Ann Reed, sung to the melody of "Diamonds Are a Girl's Best Friend," by Jule Styne.

A kiss on the hand may be quite long in coming,
Power tools are a girl's best friend.
A kiss may be grand but it won't fix the plumbing
In your humble flat or help install a second bath.
Boys get weird when girls appear
With their tool belts and drills in their hands.
Cordless screwdrivers, jigsaws and miters,
Power tools are a girl's best friend.

Like recessive genes this will show up for certain,
Power tools are a girl's best friend.
It all seems routine maybe hanging a curtain,
and this simple chore will send her to a hardware store,
Lumber yards; I've got my Home Depot card,
And you'll find that the search never ends.
Pneumatic hammers and orbital sanders,
Power tools are a girl's best friend.

Copyright Ann Reed, from her 1997 album *Timing Is Everything* (A Major Label—www.annreed.com) and used by permission.

A veteran Montana father once told me that he didn't let his daughters move away from home until they knew how to successfully:

- Drive a stick shift
- Change a tire
- Use power tools

Of course, if your daughter or stepdaughter is learning to drive or already has her license, you should be sure she masters the first two items. She can learn the last item on the list even before she starts driving.

By the time she's halfway through high school, every girl should know how to safely and effectively use basic household power tools like a circular saw, drill, sander, jigsaw, and router. If you have many trees in your yard and/or use a woodstove, she should also know how to safely use a chain saw and ax—and know how to split wood (wear those safety glasses).

Tools are invaluable when tackling a project. But any tool can also cause serious harm if not used carefully. So always drill home (no pun intended) the lesson that tools must be treated with respect.

Don't start teaching power tool use until your daughter is developmentally ready, usually around age twelve, and then allow only limited use under your close supervision. When she's about fifteen she can probably handle more responsibility, but still with your supervision close at hand. (By the way, these same rules apply to sons, too.)

Here are the absolute must rules for power tool usage
(no matter how old you are):

- Always wear safety goggles when using electrical power tools.
- Pick the right tool for the job.
- Wear personal protective equipment such as earplugs when operating loud equipment, and a dust mask when sawing, drilling, or sweeping.
- Make sure all cords are always in good repair.
- Replace or repair damaged tools or cords.
- Make sure all safety shields are in good shape to protect users from flying debris and moving parts.
- Keep the area around tools free from clutter to prevent falls.

Adapted from tips from the nonprofit organization Farm Safety 4 Just Kids (www.fs4jk.org).

All tools pose some amount of danger, but electric hand tools have the added danger of speed, power, and electrical currents that can shock and even kill when not used properly. That's why teaching the safe and proper use of nonpowered hand tools is a good first step to take before moving on to safe power tool use. See the "Toolbox" activity (p. 100) for more about that.

As you work with your daughter, make sure to bring a generous supply of patience. She's never done this before, and it will take time for her to learn the basics (try to remember how long it took you to master the skills). Get her comfortable using slightly less dangerous tools like drills and sanders before moving on to routers and saws.

Start by doing the simplest tasks on a piece of scrap wood, after clearing all staples, nails, and screws from it. For example, clamp down a clean scrap of two-by-four and have her measure different spots to drill holes, or use clean scrap to practice running the router down the sides.

To learn to use a power saw, use pieces of tightly secured (and clear) scrap wood to teach simple crosscuts on a one-by-two or two-by-four. Repeat these practice cuts until you are completely convinced that she is treating the tools with respect, putting safety first, and understanding the basics of making a clean cut that comes out to the desired length.

Of course, the best way to generate ongoing excitement about power tool use (and most other skills) is to do it in the course of a larger, interesting enterprise—like building a bookshelf, workbench, table, or any of a hundred other things you can imagine.

A great project to start with is a simple two-shelf bookshelf. It requires only five pieces of wood and can be constructed without fancy techniques like mitering, rabbets, biscuits, and all those other things that Norm Abram makes look so easy on PBS's *New Yankee Workshop*. The girl-edited *New Moon: The Magazine for Girls and Their Dreams* has just such a straightforward (and girl-designed) bookshelf project; you can download it for less than three dollars through a link on the *Dads & Daughters Togetherness Guide* website (see website, p. 168).

Through the years, I've built several simple things like bookshelves and spice racks in the basement with my department-store, handheld power tools. I've never mastered the finer points of woodworking; so, for example, my projects have screws and nails where Norm's have biscuits and dowels. As a result, my screw-heads and low tolerance for sanding are visible (if you're the type that goes around looking for that kind of thing on furniture at other people's houses), but the pieces are just as functional as Norm's. Plus, I can assure your daughter and you that a dark wood stain forgives many woodworking sins.

If you are more ambitious and skilled than I am, you and your daughter can take on larger projects. For example, try the lovely two-part bookcase for which *American Woodworker* magazine's website supplies free drawings, instructions, and a materials list. If, like me, you two have more ambition than skill, tackle this project anyway. The drawing (www.rd.com/americanwoodworker/articles/200009/bookcase/page2.ht ml) shows where you're supposed to use biscuits—feel free to substitute good wood screws and wood glue instead.

American Woodworker provides other free (but fairly advanced) plans along with guidance on power tool techniques. Several projects (like a keepsake box and a hockey table) are great fun to do with your daughter. Visit www.rd.com/americanwoodworker.

With a little digging online, you can find free patterns and instructions for a number of woodworking projects. Here are some I uncovered:

> Doghouse: www.woodzone.com/plans/doghouse/doghouse_
>   plans.htm
> Hanging porch swing: www.buildeazy.com/porchswing_1.html
> Playhouse: www.buildeazy.com/wendyhouse_imp.html
> Jigsaw puzzles (simple, for small children):
> www.instantplans.com/free_scrollsaw_patterns.html

I found the widest selection of free plans in one place at the Build-Eazy website: www.buildeazy.com/fp_start.html

Tip: In our culture, many of us (including dads) still have blind spots about the capabilities and interests of girls and women. It is extremely hard for anyone to explore their capabilities and interests in a skill if they are never exposed to activities that make use of that skill. That's why it's so important for stepfathers and fathers to expose our daughters to pursuits—like sports, building, woodworking, home repair, science—that are not "traditionally" seen as being female endeavors.

Share photos and stories about the projects you build on the *Dads & Daughters Togetherness Guide* website (see website, p. 168).

47. Fast Fun for Daughters Years Fourteen and Up

Fourteen to Eighteen / Solo

When you have a teenager, it can sometimes seem impossible to think of things to do together. However, teens are often capable of doing a wider variety of activities than younger girls. The key is hitting on something that will get her (and you) psyched about participating together.

This Fast Fun list is only the beginning of what's possible. Be creative and keep an open mind; you'll find there are hundreds of additional fun things to do side-by-side with your teen daughter.

Snow ski.

Water ski.

Talk about the future.

Go to a concert together.

Hunt.

Fish.

Play checkers or chess.

Take a long hike.

Listen to her stories about school.

Explore the Internet together.

Just the two of you go to a restaurant once a month.

Go to a fireworks display.

Go to the movies together (Dad buys the popcorn and Daughter picks the movie).

Shop together for clothes, sports equipment, school supplies, books, etc.

Bake a pie (more challenging than a cake).

Plan and take a trip together.

Paint the house (or part of it) together.

Listen to her music.

48. *Top Ten List*
Fourteen to Eighteen / Solo

Sometimes we're so busy trying to get through today's crazed schedule—and preparing for tomorrow's and the next day's—that we forget to talk about the most important things. This is a simple exercise in taking the time to do just that.

Top Ten List is designed for older girls, as they near the age when they will be leaving the nest and setting off to create their own lives. It uses that "flying-off" day as the motivation for completing the lists.

In the first list, Dad writes what he wants his stepdaughter and/or daughter to know before she leaves home—skills, concepts, things about himself—while Daughter writes about who she is, what she believes, what her world is like.

In the second list, each of you asks about things you've always wondered about the other person: dreams, passions, and/or practical talents.

Father and daughter each make a Top Ten List that relates to the other person. Don't share your lists with each other until both of you are completely finished writing them.

Under each list, I've made suggestions of the type of things a person might list—but don't feel restricted by my suggestions. The lists can include anything, so be creative.

However, it helps to include items that are important to your heart and your relationship with each other.

A. The Top Ten Things I Want You to Know Before You/I Grow Up and Move Away

Dad might list:

I will always love you.
How to use power tools (see p. 149).
Disappointment doesn't have to defeat you.
How proud I am when you _____.

Daughter might list:

I will always love you.
I can handle mistakes.
How to make friendship bracelets (see p. 104).
How to understand soccer.

B. The Top Ten Things I Want to Know about You Before You/I Leave Home

Dad might list:

What you value most in a friend.
Of all the people who died before you were born, who would you
    most like to meet?
What does loyalty mean to you?
How you paint so well.

Daughter might list:

Why you chose the work you did.
How you manage money and why (see p. 108).
Of all the people who died before you were born, who would you
    most like to meet?
How I changed you as a person.

When completed, share your lists with each other and talk about what you each chose to write. You don't have to answer every question or discuss every item the first time around. And you don't have to drop a subject just because you discussed it already. If the lists stimulate ongoing conversations, that's just great.

You and your daughter can do this activity in one sitting, or you can decide to take more time (even as much as a week) to finish it.

Be sure to keep your lists (and any reflection on them) in your DDPJ (see p. 24). And feel free to do this activity more than once. Over the course of the years, your answers will change because each of you is changing—so there are always new things to learn about each other.

Also, explore other topics that can generate Top Ten Lists to discuss. You might try subjects like "The Top Ten Qualities of the Person I Admire Most in the World" or "The Top Ten Struggles I've Faced in My Life So Far" and whatever else you create.

Tip: As written, this exercise deals with abstract concepts, so it is best suited for girls at more advanced developmental stages. However, feel free to adapt it for younger stepdaughters and daughters, making the lists more concrete and related to her developmental level.

49. Fast Fun: Places

All Ages / Solo and Group

Fast Fun is a list of activity ideas that a father can pull out anytime. They don't require a lot of preparation or explanation. But if you're stumped for ideas of what to do today or this coming weekend, scan this list and you'll find a place to go that you both can enjoy.

Local drag races (bring earplugs).
Batting cage.
Driving range.
Bowling alley.
Video arcade.
Tennis court.
Library.
The beach.
The annual home show (or boat show, RV/camping show, etc.).
Mud puddle (get in old clothes and slop around during or after a rainstorm).
Miniature golf.
Piles of raked leaves (jump up and down, build forts, throw them high and shout).
Ice-skating rink.
The front porch (to watch a thunderstorm do its thing, or gaze at the sky).
The driveway (to wash the car or change the oil together).

Tip: Men and women often communicate differently. That includes dads and daughters. Females tend to show they care by sharing words and conversations about emotions and relationships. Males tend to show they care by sharing space and time, in other words, being near people they love and/or doing good things for and with them. It's important for Dad to stretch himself and communicate on his daughter's terms. But it's also important to respect and value the power and legitimacy of how Dad shows his love through sharing space and time together.

50. *Straight Talks*
Fourteen to Eighteen / Solo

When my twin daughters were teenagers, I regularly felt stumped by them. After talking to veteran fathers (and hearing my wife talk about being a teen with her parents), I realized that I wasn't alone. Every stepfather and father has baffled moments.

But that knowledge didn't always make things better. The Straight Talk activity is aimed at helping you overcome what I called "Five Hurdles for Fathers of Daughters" in my book *Dads & Daughters: How to Inspire, Understand, and Support Your Daughter.*

Hurdle #1: We grew up as boys. We simply have no experience in what it's like to grow up as a girl.

Hurdle #2: We're stereotyped. Our culture sees fathers as either invisible, incompetent, second-class parents, or as all-knowing Cosby Show superheroes. In reality, all of us fall somewhere in between.

Hurdle #3: The Protector Predicament. It's hard to balance our desire to protect our daughters from danger with our need to allow them to handle difficulty, survive mistakes, and learn to trust themselves.

Hurdle #4: The Provider Predicament. We must help provide for our families—but not equate that responsibility solely with what's in our wallet. We must also provide our time, attention, masculinity, affection, tolerance for risk, experience—in other words, our whole selves.

Hurdle #5: The Silence of the Dads. Fathers seldom talk to other fathers about raising a girl. Plus, did your father ever speak to you

*about how he grew as a man by having you as his son? We must be-
gin breaking that cycle of silence.*

Throughout the *Dads & Daughters Togetherness Guide,* we've been emphasizing the importance of listening to daughters. Listening to girls is the primary way of clearing the hurdles of fathering daughters. An effective way to "listen to girls" is by having Straight Talk conversations. Those are conversations when we summon up the courage to speak directly to each other with our thoughts and questions while keeping an open mind and a loving attitude that invites frank responses.

Here are a few questions to get you started in a Straight Talk conversation with your teenage daughter or stepdaughter (both of you should feel free to add to this list):

What do you wish we had more ability or time to do together?
What do you wish you had more ability or time to do for yourself?
What do you wish I had more ability or time to do for myself?
What is your greatest joy in life today?
What is your greatest concern about our relationship?
What's the most important thing that you think we should be talking about that we haven't been talking about—or else are not talking enough about?
When we're together, what topics am I hoping you won't mention, and what topics are you hoping I won't broach?
How can I help you get where you want to go?
If you could stop doing something right now, what would it be?
What gives you the greatest satisfaction today? The greatest pride?

As the father, you must set the tone of Straight Talks. That means actively listening and being willing to sit through silences; silences that may feel excruciating in the moment, but which can draw out the deepest feelings, thoughts, and insights.

We called this Straight Talks (plural) intentionally. It is crucial not to limit discussion of important life issues to one Capital "T" Talk (like the traditional One Big Talk about the birds and the bees). Straight Talks help both of you have numerous lower-case "t" talks in which you share your values through ongoing everyday conversations.

The purpose of Straight Talks is not to lecture, pass judgment, or shower our daughters with every bit of wisdom we've accumulated in life. Instead, the purpose is to shower her with the powerful tonic, light, nourishment, and comfort of our attention—by listening respectfully and taking her seriously.

Believe it or not, your stepdaughter or daughter knows a lot about her world and probably knows a fair amount about who she is. In some areas, her knowledge of her self and her world may be greater than yours. You have much to learn from her. That doesn't change the fact that she also has much to learn from you. That kind of mutual learning happens best when you make listening priority number one.

> **Tip:** Jot down your reflections, feelings, thoughts, and other insights after having one of your Straight Talks—and do it before you go to sleep that night. Save those jottings in a private place or in your DDPJ (see p. 24). Those words may end up teaching you new things about your daughter and yourself for years to come.

51. *Big Bike Ride*
Thirteen to Eighteen-Plus / Solo or Group

After my daughter Nia was finished with her high school years, she started planning a major trip: riding her bicycle around Lake Superior with two friends. Lake Superior has the largest surface area of any freshwater lake in the world—and a ride around it covers close to a thousand miles of road. I was jealous!

Somebody once asked Nia what got her so interested in bike-riding, and she said it was riding with me on the rural Willard Munger bike trail at the edge of our hometown. She said her proudest memory of that trail was riding faster and farther than me.

Distance bicycle-riding is physically demanding, but more forgiving than many other endurance sports (like marathon running). It allows people with different physical capabilities to share the same physical activity. Biking also works just as well for groups of father-daughter pairs as it does for just one pair on their own. No matter where or how you go biking, remember that no one (adults included) sets foot on pedal without securely attaching their bike helmet first.

Daylong Trip

The first thing to know is that you shouldn't set off for a half-day or full-day bike adventure without building up your stamina and flexibility first. Make absolutely sure that stretching exercises are a continuing part of your training regimen. If you try to do an eight-hour ride after not picking up your bike for years, you will sorely regret it (in all senses of that adjective).

Pick a low-traffic route to travel because it is safer and quieter, which makes it easier to chat while riding. Many states have converted abandoned railroad right-of-ways into dedicated bike paths, which are ideal for trips of a few hours or more.

Arrange your logistics carefully—either ride a loop so you return to your starting point, or arrange for someone to meet you at the end point and transport you and the equipment home.

Be sure to carry enough water and energy sources to more than cover your needs. So-called camelback water devices (basically a bladder inside a knapsack) or sufficient water bottles are essential.

Carry snacks, including protein sources (nuts, cheese sticks) and energy sources (candy bars). Skip anything salty! If going on an all-day ride, bring two light "picnic" meals you can eat during breaks.

The best father-daughter bike rides focus on the scenery and the time together, not on racing. If there is a significant difference in biking ability and stamina (and the advantage isn't always Dad's!), build that into your approach. If you love bird-watching, wildlife, or wild plants, bring along binoculars and an identifier book. The stronger rider should always (patiently) let the weaker one set the pace, so both parties enjoy the experience.

The National Highway Traffic Safety Administration has a kid-oriented website (www.nhtsa.dot.gov/kids/biketour/) on bicycle safety—a good place for both of you to visit.

Overnight Trips (and Longer Adventures)

If you are avid riders, or become avid riders, going on an overnight trip is the ultimate thrill. Of course, staying overnight on the trail usually means carrying a fair amount of gear with you—like a tent, sleeping bags, cookstove, food, rain gear, sufficient water, and so on.

The best approach is to prepare by riding some or all of your ultimate route in smaller chunks, so that you can plot out together where you want to stop for meals and camping. If your route will take you through large enough towns at the right time of day, you can opt for staying in a motel rather than a tent (because most tents lack hot showers).

Consult with a bike shop on how to outfit your bike with the proper mounting and balancing of carrying equipment like panniers, baskets, bags, and the like. The bike shop's professionals can also guide you on getting the right kind of lights, pedals, shoes, and other gear for the route you're taking and the weather you're likely to encounter.

Obviously, the logistics and supplies for overnight and longer bike adventures are exponentially more complex than those needed for a Sunday afternoon meander. So be conservative. Start with shorter trips so you discover your personal rhythms, likes, dislikes, and needs. Think of this as research for making a longer trip later on.

For a longer adventure (something on the order of riding around a Great Lake), start training about four months in advance. You should have 300 to 600 miles of training rides *per month,* but you can substitute hours on a stationary bike for some of those miles (about five minutes on a stationary bike equals one mile of road training). Make absolutely sure that stretching exercises are a continuing part of your training regimen.

After building a good training base, start riding in hilly terrain to develop your strength and rhythm. Next, start building endurance by taking long rides a couple of times a week, so that by about six weeks before your trip, you can cover 40 to 50 miles a day. During the last six weeks, start adding weight to your bike to prepare for hauling the food and equipment you'll need to camp out for days and weeks at a time.

The Adventure Cycling Association website (www.adv-cycling.org/index.cfm) has training and equipment tips, maps and routes for bike trails across North America, ways to hook up with fellow bikers, and much more. You can also make use of commercial bike tour providers, like Experience Plus (www.experienceplus.com), which supply logistical support and routes around the world.

52. Communication Game
Thirteen to Eighteen-Plus / Solo

Did you notice the secret subtext in each of this book's activities? Each of the previous activities is designed to facilitate easier communication between you and your daughter and/or stepdaughter. Open communication builds trust, and trust is the glue of any solid human bond.

However, trust is a tricky thing, especially for the stepfather or father who has a daughter approaching or careening through adolescence. Too many teen girls and adult women say that their father pulled away during their adolescence, leaving them feeling betrayed—and betrayal eats through trust like acid.

We dads are sometimes tempted to pull away because our adolescent stepdaughters and daughters sometimes act like—well, let's be honest—brats. But even when our feelings are deeply hurt by their outbursts or obnoxious behavior, we need to stay connected and loyal to our girls. It is at those hurt and "I feel stuck" times that simple shared activity and communication tools can save the day.

Throughout the *Dads & Daughters Togetherness Guide,* you've seen conversation-starter questions on cards. These are actually game pieces in a brilliant entertainment developed by California dad and accountant Gary Burns (with quite a bit of help from his two daughters, Jessica and Sophie).

Gary's game, Com-mu-ni-ca-tion—Dads & Daughters Edition, is designed specifically for fathers and daughters to break the ice and stimulate interesting discussions. The best part of the game, however, is that it sets up a regular schedule for you to take your daughter out for one-on-one time—and then gives both of you something to talk about!

After being overseas for his daughter Jessica's fourteenth, fifteenth, and sixteenth birthdays, Gary realized that the relationship was truly more important than any kudos he got at work. So he decided to start "dating" Jessica once a month—going out alone with her to a restaurant and getting to know her better. For fun, he suggested working through the alphabet, so the first date was breakfast at Applebee's.

With great anticipation, Gary and Jessica sat down in a booth. But after ordering their meals, they had difficulty maintaining a conversation, and the long silent pauses were painfully awkward. Sound familiar?

So, before they set off the following month to the Bon Ami Café (next letter in the alphabet), Gary wrote out a homemade game with fourteen thin slips of paper upon which he'd written fourteen statements, such as: "I really like it when you and I _____. I say that because . . ." Throughout the meal, Jessica and Gary took turns unwrapping the fourteen pieces of paper and answering the statements. An hour and a half later the final statement was answered and the "date" was a complete success. They laughed, thought hard, shared openly, and gained important new insights about each other.

After years of inventing and testing with Jessica, her sister Sophie, and other father-daughter pairs, Gary now has a professionally produced and handsomely packaged game—with 365 questions!

You can learn more about Com-mu-ni-ca-tion—Dads & Daughters Edition at www.mindamics.com. You can purchase a copy there, or get one as part of your membership in the national Dads & Daughters nonprofit at www.dadsanddaughters.org. This game is an outstanding and fun activity that can last for years—well into adulthood!

Even if you forgo Gary's game, don't forgo the incredible opportunity to step with your daughter or stepdaughter into the sacred space of "just the two of us" time together. The dozens of activities in this book can help ease your way into that time of talk, trust, and true connection. What the two of you do with your very special bond now (and for the rest of your lives) will amaze you.

Enjoy the ride!

53. Togetherness Guide *Website*
All Ages / Solo and Group

The national nonprofit Dads & Daughters is the force behind this book. Dads & Daughters members sent us so many ideas from all around the country that we couldn't fit them all in one book.

That's why we created a special part of our website, dedicated to fun activities that dads do with their daughters and stepdaughters. In this activity, I encourage you and your daughter to visit that website for two reasons:

1. To learn about additional activities that can build fun and lasting memories for both of you.
2. To contribute ideas of your own—and memories of the times you did activities in this *Dads & Daughters Togetherness Guide*.

Visit the *Dads & Daughters Togetherness Guide* section of the Dads & Daughters website at www.dadsanddaughters.org/for-everyone/Togetherness-Guide.aspx. You'll find a place to submit your stories, artwork, and photos. You can also find dozens of new ideas for father-daughter activities submitted by others—and submit new ideas yourselves.

Also, be sure to visit Dads & Daughters (www.dadsanddaughters.org) and the website of our periodical *Daughters®: For Parents of Girls* (www.daughters.com) for their many tips, resources, and news items to help you build a fun, strong, and lasting relationship with your stepdaughter and/or daughter.

54. Activity Jar
All Ages / Solo

We've designed the next few pages to help you make a *Dads & Daughters Togetherness Guide* jar. As you can see, they list each activity in the *Togetherness Guide* (along with the page where you can find it) in a small box. Photocopy the pages, and then cut out each one of the boxes. You will end up with small slips of paper that you can fold in half, so that the words are hidden. Put all of the slips of paper into a large jar, and then store the jar in a visible location (like the kitchen counter).

When it comes time for father-daughter play, have your daughter or stepdaughter shake up the jar, reach in, and pick out an activity. Then go ahead and do that activity. If she isn't in the mood for that one, let her reach back in and grab another, but it's a good idea to limit the number of times she gets a do-over. (Thanks to Grace and Cora's brilliant dad Steve Knauss for creating this idea.)

Acknowledgments

The *Dads & Daughters Togetherness Guide* owes a huge debt to Bill Klatte of Wisconsin, Scott MacGregor of North Carolina, and Bob Stien of New York, dads who shared copious notes and ideas on how they play with their daughters. Much of the "Fast Fun" information was generously contributed by Bill from his fabulous book *Live-Away Dads: Staying a Part of Your Children's Lives When They Aren't a Part of Your Home* (Penguin, 1999).

The men of the Dads & Daughters online discussion group and other fathers in the Dads & Daughters network contributed dozens of ideas based on their own experience; they include Eric Ewald, Adam Lantheaume, Andre Schayk, Bob Sands, Bryon Giddens, Chris DeMotta, Chuck Kaiser, Dan Meyer, Dave Moffat, David Drewes, Dave Powers, Dennis Austin, Devin Lowe, Joe Oca, Joel Rice, Marc Mortinson, Michael Petrucelli, Michael Werner, Peter Matthews, Robert Kehle, Sam Weinstein, Thomas Zucker, and Phillip Rodriguez.

Some adult daughters—including Robin Dellabough, Rosalie Maggio, Kim Lund, Carol Harris, Melody Morrell, and Diane Creston—shared fun activities they did with their dads and/or kids. My own now-adult daughters, Nia Kelly and Mavis Gruver, also invented some entertainments that found their way into this book. In addition, Mavis and Nia introduced me to new levels of fun (and love) during their childhood, for which I feel everlasting gratitude.

Special thanks to Grace and Cora Knauss's father Steve for his priceless insights on getting fathers over a daughter's resistance to playing with Dad, and to Gary, Jessica, and Sophie Burns for sharing game cards from their fabulous Com-mu-ni-ca-tion—Dads & Daughters Edition game (www.mindamics.com).

Deep thanks to the board of directors of the national nonprofit Dads & Daughters: Rev. Steve Emmett, Ph.D.; Margo Maine, Ph.D.; Eric Ewald; Rev. Galen Guengerich, Ph.D.; Laurie Harbert, Scott

MacGregor, and Bob Stien; honorary members Geena Davis and Michael Kieschnick, Ph.D.; and former member David Sadker, Ed.D.

Many thanks to Carren W. Joye of www.onlineplaygroup.com, Shari Burgus of Farm Safety 4 Just Kids (www.fs4jk.org), Dr. Judy Shoaf of the University of Florida, and Rich Snowdon for permission to adapt some of their resources for this guide. Thanks to Ann Reed for permission to reprint the lyrics to her song "Power Tools." Just to cover all the legal bases, I acknowledge myself for granting permission to adapt material from my book *Dads & Daughters: How to Inspire, Understand, and Support Your Daughter* (Broadway, 2003), copyright 2002, all rights reserved.

My editors, Trish Medved and Becky Cole, and I had good fun working on this project, which is only appropriate for a book about play. I thank them for their enthusiasm and guidance. I've written previously about the privilege of having Robin Dellabough for an agent. It is an even greater privilege to have her as a friend.

Many thanks to Lisa Oakman (www.lisaoakman.com) who volunteered to grace this book with her illustrations. She went above and beyond the call and we're eternally grateful.

I also appreciate the support of Helen Cordes, editor of *Daughters: For Parents of Girls* (www.daughters.com), as well as the dedicated, smart, and delightful people who work for Dads & Daughters, including Ann Miller, Melody Morrell, and Nancy Gruver. I have the additional good fortune of being married to Nancy, who is my chief scout and interpreter in the often mysterious world of daughters.

This book is dedicated to Michael Kieschnick, the father who created Dads & Daughters in 1999, when there was no organization dedicated to the power and potential of relationships between daughters and their fathers and stepfathers. That was also a time when public conversation was virtually silent on the importance of this unique family bond. Inspired by his children Jordan and Hannah, Michael founded an organization to shatter that silence. The rest of us are benefiting from the wave of awareness and learning he sparked. So, as you use this book to have fun with—and grow closer to—your daughter or stepdaughter, remember to thank her for the honor of being her dad; and then shout out some gratitude to Michael Kieschnick, too.

Index

About the Author

Former journalist JOE KELLY is co-founder of Dads & Daughters—the national organization dedicated to making the world safe and fair for our daughters—and the author of *Dads & Daughters: How to Inspire, Understand, and Support Your Daughter*. He is also the father of twin adult daughters. His work has been extensively featured in the media, including NPR, NBC, CBS, ABC, *People, USA Today,* and the *New York Times*. He was awarded the 1995 Parenting Achievement Award from *Parenting* magazine and helped his wife, Nancy Gruver, launch *New Moon*, the award-winning international magazine edited by girls. He lives in St. Paul, Minnesota.